AT THIS TIME, IN THIS PLACE

AT THIS TIME, IN THIS PLACE

THE SPIRIT EMBODIED IN THE LOCAL ASSEMBLY

MICHAEL WARREN

TRINITY PRESS INTERNATIONAL
Harrisburg, Pennsylvania

BX
1746
.W36
1999

Trinity Press International, P.O. Box 1321, Harrisburg, PA 17105
Trinity Press International is a division of the Morehouse Group

Library of Congress Cataloging-in-Publication Data
Warren, Michael, 1935-
    At this time, in this place : the spirit embodied in the local
assembly / Michael Warren.
        p.   cm.
    Includes bibliographical references and index.
    ISBN 1-56338-251-2 (pbk. : alk. paper)
    1. Church renewal – Catholic Church.   I. Title.
BX1746.W36 1999
250 – dc 21   99-11285

Printed in the United States of America

99   00   01   02   03   04   10   9   8   7   6   5   4   3   2   1

*This book is for those Xaverian Brothers
with whom I have lived.
By exhibiting the possibilities of gospel practice,
especially the practice of poverty,
they made this book possible.*

Contents

Acknowledgments

THE BACKGROUND STUDY for this book was done during a sabbatical year in 1992–93, given to me by colleagues and administrators at St. John's University. However, what made that full year of study financially possible was a study grant from the Lilly Endowment, for which I remain deeply grateful. That Lilly grant (and the encouragement of Jim Wind that accompanied it) also made possible my various published essays on the local church that have preceded this book. St. John's Department of Theology and Religious Studies further supported the final writing and revising with a reduction in my teaching schedule in 1995–96. Colleagues in the Association of Professors and Researchers in Religious Education who reacted to "research papers" that I presented at its annual meetings provided encouragement to keep writing at times when I was unsure I was on the right course. Perhaps most helpful were the students in my graduate catechetical courses at St. John's, whose responses to various chapters were probing and heartening. I cannot omit here R. Kevin Seasoltz, O.S.B., editor of *Worship*, and John Pawlikowski, O.S.M., editor of *New Theology Review*, who saw fit to publish versions of these chapters in their journals.

Others who read and reacted to either chapters or versions of the entire book are Marianne Sawicki, C. Ellis Nelson, Michael-Paul Gallagher, S.J., and Herman Lombaerts. Patrick Primeaux, S.M., and Pamela Kirk of our St. John's University Department of Theology and Religious Studies offered detailed suggestions for revision, as did Robin Maas of Washington, D.C., Robert Kinast, the director of the Center for Theological Reflection in Florida, and Alfred Hennelly, S.J., of Fordham. Anne E. Patrick, S.N.J.M., gave the final manuscript a keen review and made many helpful comments. All along, my most faithful and pointed questioners have been Don Kraus and Connie Loos. At St. John's crucial help was given to this project by Frances Fico, who labored over the initial index and bibliography with her usual efficiency and wonderful disposition. Of all the above help, hers was the most indispensable.

To these friends and colleagues who provided the "material conditions" needed for this book, I say, "Many thanks."

Introduction

EDUCATIONAL PSYCHOLOGIST Shoshana Felman notes that every learning situation is marked by two characteristics, one of which is usually recognized and the other of which is usually overlooked. The first characteristic is those things the learners want to know. Ordinarily learners consciously embrace these matters; they know what they want to know. The second characteristic, which provides a distinct challenge in all learning situations, is this: those things the learners cannot afford to know or dare not let themselves know. Another way to put it: they have an active interest in — no, a passionate interest in — not knowing.[1]

The second characteristic does not arise from the rational and mind-driven goal orientation of modernity. Instead, it surges out of affectively based aversions that run outside of conscious control. I suspect there may be some ideas in this book that readers may not want to let themselves know or think about. To the extent this proves true, the book reproduces in readers the struggles I myself have had in writing it. I had to get past my own aversions, my own unwillingness to stare; what helped was recognizing the consequences of not facing specific problems and challenges. The church too suffers consequences when it refuses to pay focused attention to its own life.

When I realized several years ago the degree to which culture is the greatest and most overlooked educational influence in most lives, making the influence of Christian education and catechesis seem like a pebble at the foot of a mountain, I set out to study the particular ways culture works. That study shifted my perspective and has influenced everything I have written since. What I came to realize was that religious groups, such as the church, are actually cultures within wider cultures. They are zones of meaning prompting their adherents to question the meanings of the wider culture. As such, religions can be healthy countervailing forces, examining, contesting, and redirecting the meanings of the wider social-economic order. Potentially at least, they provide an alternative humanizing vision of the purpose of life. I

1

tried to set out these convictions about culture in *Seeing through the Media: A Religious View of Communications and Cultural Analysis* (1997). This book is not a sequel. In many ways the issues this book raises were the intuitive origins of the decision to write *Seeing through the Media*. Whatever their sequence, both books were prompted by a sense that the churches were being successfully colonized by the wider culture. This book examines the conditions under which religious groups, particularly the Christian churches, can become embodiments of their foundational convictions about the human situation. Under what conditions can the local church so resonate with the Spirit of Jesus that others can see that it dances a different dance and to a different tune? This study also examines the conditions of contemporary culture that are hostile to religious insight and to religious practice of that insight.

Behind this book is the conviction that ideas, beliefs, and ideological moods do not spring mysteriously into the "hearts" and "souls" of persons. They become a reality — in its original meaning, *real-ized* — when made tangible in words, actions, clothing, manners, and organizations. Only by being able to poke people in the ribs, by being able to touch people in their daily living, can moods, beliefs, or philosophical views become actual and steadily able to impinge on what people understand as reality.[2] In other words, to use traditionally Christian language, hidden religious realities become actual when they are sacramental, that is, when concrete enactments touch persons in a way that opens them to the religious core of life. When a local church's life ceases to have this sacramental power to touch people religiously — or at least to raise questions for them about life itself — something terrible has happened and something vital has disappeared.

Those who study the interactions of married couples find the most telling sign of a dead relationship to be the inability or unwillingness of one or both partners to read the emotional signals of the other. Total strangers may be more adept than the spouse at understanding what the partner is saying. Emotional deafness in a relationship is a sign of emotional illness and even death. Nonresponsiveness, which often does not characterize chance meetings between total strangers, can come to characterize a relationship once intensely intimate. In such a case, something terrible has happened because a vital element has disappeared.[3] Something analogous happens to communities who lose their gospel resonance.

The Good News of Jesus calls for response, in individuals and communities. And so, when communities who have pledged their lives to the gospel are characteristically unresponsive to it, something terrible has indeed happened. As with married couples, the thing that is wrong can be more obvious to those outside the community than those inside. As I see it, flourishing love (and creativity) is characterized by both joy and nervousness: joy in who or what is loved and nervousness that it could be lost or betrayed. Healthy nervousness is the creative edge of love. I want local churches to be at least as nervous about their discipleship as I am about this book.

This book is written to foster the aliveness and responsiveness of the local church, and through it I want to celebrate the possibilities of the local church as a living sacrament of the gospel. This book is meant to be a hymn to the Spirit of Jesus tangibly present in the coming together, in a particular place and at a particular time in history, of disciples who face the challenges of that time and place. All theology exists to serve that coming together and the difference it makes. Our Scriptures are a testimony to the original fruitfulness of such assemblies, and ministry's purpose is to serve the possibilities of such living. The discipling assembly is the toe of the shoe all church leaders kneel to kiss. The local church in its inconvenient discipleship reimagines for our time the contours of the human itself. Such reimagining is salvific.

A Roman Catholic pastoral theologian, teaching at a large urban Roman Catholic university, I am very aware of my specific Roman Catholic "dialect." However my intention in doing the actual writing was to produce an interdenominational book, speaking across denominational lines about the problems all denominations currently face. If I allude to a particular Roman Catholic example, I ask readers not to think, "This isn't about me or about us; this is 'Roman Church' stuff." The irony many of us today face is that we often find our kindred souls by the kinds of questions they are asking about gospel fidelity rather than by the denominational affiliation of their local churches. Our common brotherhood and sisterhood of discipleship is what joins us in the Spirit of Jesus.

Though written to foster aliveness, this book is not a search for a "perfect" community, a full embodiment of the gospel. Those seeking a formula for such perfection should stop right here, as this is not the book for them. Such communities do not exist. All we can have are communities struggling for a living discipleship in their own particular local circumstances. The struggle for religious coherence and integrity is what produces a life structure effectively resonating with the Good News preached by Jesus. The purpose of that struggle, I wish to emphasize, is not "success" in producing some idealized church but fidelity to the call of God, in whose Spirit we dwell.[4]

Neither is this book a fully systematic treatment of the problems of local church practice today. Taking what I consider to be the largely unrecognized problem of the church domesticated by culture, I try to view that problem from a series of angles. By this strategy I hope to foster questioning and further reflection on the problem of the church in culture. The problem cannot be worked out by following formulaic strategies. If the problem is a sclerotic practice, the solution is a re-newed practice — probing, questioning, experimenting, vivifying — by groups within an ecclesia, trying to find their way a step at a time.[5] When enough persons see the problem, renewal can begin small and proceed. However, the process will never be completed in the sense of producing a product. The process itself is the issue, luring people ever deeper into the shaping of spirit and life that necessarily accompanies the process. No book can resolve the problems of working through such a process. All it can do is expose some of these problems, suggest why they should be faced, and invite further reflection on them.[6]

At all points in this book, readers will find I keep returning to the place of worship, the Eucharist assembly. At first this anchoring in wor-ship was strategic. I thought to myself: many cannot hear questions about the life of the local church because they are convinced, implicitly maybe, that what they do in worship is the complete act of discipleship. If I can show how significant for worship are the decisions, images, and practices seeming to have nothing to do with worship, then I can get the attention of those who prize worship. The significant sacramental-ity of the community's wider life is less easily overlooked when shown to be a *condition* of the sacramentality of bread and wine and of the Lord's presence in worship. In short, if you want congregational change, you must show its significance for worship, which is one of the reasons feminists pressing for church renewal pay so much attention to worship.

Eventually I saw in my strategic focus on worship something seminal about my entire project. The issue at the heart of local congregational renewal is the coherence of a life of practice. Only when liturgi-cal speech (word and action), meant to be self-implicating, actually implicates the assembly in a search for a deeper practice of disciple-ship does the community become coherent. Worship's validation is the community's coherent life practice.

This book was not mapped out in a logical plan that I followed to its conclusion. Actually I began to deal with aspects of the problem as I saw them at particular moments. Most of the work at the beginning was to clarify the problem for myself first. Only afterwards could I attempt clarifying the issues for others.

Chapters 1, 3, and 5 deal basically with the same question — What are the practices of the local church? — but each from an increasingly wider circumference while using a more closely focused lens. These chapters evolved as I came to recognize these wider areas a bit at a time. Chapter 1 dwells on two basic matters: the credibility of the worshiping assembly and the open question of whether that assembly actually embodies the gospel. Here readers are introduced to issues like vision, life structure, practice, and stance. It is more descriptive than diagnostic. Chapter 3 carries forward the issues of the first chapter by focusing on the material conditions of a local church as a way of getting at — in a more diagnostic vein — specifics of what we do. In examining the conditions under which a local church can become aware of its own life structure and then work to change what needs to be changed, this chapter pays considerable attention to liberation theology's concern for practice and its critique of oppressive social structures, including social class. Chapter 5 takes yet another look at the material conditions of life structure, becoming at the same time more specific about them but looking at them from the perspective of social science. Readers who have ventured this far will find they face choices and decisions about what they do in both their domestic lives and in their ecclesial ones.

Chapters 2 and 4 weave new issues into the fundamental question woven and rewoven into chapters 1, 3, and 5. Chapter 2 deals with how our ways of seeing and perceiving are shaped by the "image culture" in which we live. This chapter is particularly important because of its attempt to call attention to, not matters we ourselves control, but matters that control us. Highlighted here is the fact that as Christians we have our own foundational sets of images, tied to our Jesus-inspired tradition, that fundamentally contradict much of our current image culture. Chapter 4 is about speech in our churches, about who speaks and under what conditions, about what the power to speak says to ordinary churchgoers regarding their own ability to speak from a gospel perspective. Although the entire book is about church renewal, this chapter raises the issues about authority, judgment, and participation that are best addressed by long-range pastoral strategies.

The final chapter is about the notion of practice and how specific practices can enliven a local church. It came from a desire, in the end, to specify certain procedures (practices) of the local church. My hope is that it will round out for readers the understandings of the preceding five chapters.

In summary, the social context in which faith is being lived today and which is shaping the spirits of Christian people tends to function outside our awareness. How is it possible to develop communal skills of reflection, judgment or discernment, and decision needed for gospel fidelity in our time? Though the chapters of this book offer various ways of getting at this question, I myself have no simple answer. Indeed, the question is not easily answered — and in my view cannot be dealt with solely via programmatic instructional strategies. Whatever is done will happen at the level of the speech of all the people and the action of the communal body. Reimagining the possibilities of the local church is a large part of the challenge.

This book might best be read communally or collaboratively with a group of others willing to think about discipleship in a time of massive media manipulation. Margaret Miles is right in warning that we live in an entertainment culture, bent on assigning us roles as spectators or passive voyeurs, whose role in the end is to say either "I liked it" or "I didn't like it" and whose own core of judgment has been slowly but surely eroded.[7] Since the questions probed in these pages are not little ones, the context allowing them to be fruitfully faced, evaluated, and, in all likelihood, recast might well be some sort of circle of discourse. That is why I have added at the end of each of the first five chapters questions that pastoral staffs, discussion groups, or pastoral councils might use as a basis for discussion. After all, as its title suggests, this book's issue is not things in general but discipleship in particular places and times and with particular persons.

This book's amorphous genre will be a problem to some. Is it a book about Christian education/catechesis or pastoral ministry or liturgy or ethics or culture or modernity or communications? It is about all of these things and none of them, as it has to be in order to get at the dilemmas of the contemporary church. Genres aside, if this book opens readers to a problem often overlooked and summons them to work at communal discipleship, I will be pleased.

Possibly the genre of this book is "reflection on theology as actionable or practicable." It is an exercise in practical theology and an attempt to highlight its importance today. It is written in response to a catechetical issue: the life of the local church as the great communicator of the gospel. My "nervous" hope is that it will be helpful.

CHAPTER ONE

THE WORSHIPING ASSEMBLY
Zone of Cultural Contestation

THIS CHAPTER, indeed this entire book, explores a catechetical or Christian education question but does so in categories that may not seem connected to catechesis. I hesitate to state my purpose in this way because so many see catechesis as marginal to theology and to the deepest issues of church reform. In some university theology programs, teachers assume that doctrinal history, doctrinal analysis, and biblical studies are essential for a theologian's repertoire; catechesis and related pastoral studies are not "academic" but merely the application of theology. I take an opposite view. Whenever and wherever theology loses its moorings in actual local communities of practice and ceases to be attentive to what people are actually living, it drifts off into an intellectual void. Worse, the communities themselves face the loss of their own sacramentality, that is, of their life as a credible sign of God's presence.

The reasons catechesis has been so badly understood or even misconceived in the church are readily understandable. In some denominations, centuries of question-and-answer catechesis are partly to blame; in others, Christian education seems to have little intellectual or even spiritual depth. However, at the heart of the renewal of theology in our century were serious catechetical matters that still jump out at us from the pages penned in the thirties by Karl Rahner, Henri de Lubac, and Josef Jungmann.[1] Those interested in understanding the theological goals of Karl Barth and Rudolf Bultmann dare not forget that both brought from their chaplaincies in World War I urgent pastoral questions to their theological reflection. Events of their pastoral work with young soldiers implicated them in deep pastoral theological questions.

In my view the area still lagging behind in the renewal of theology today is the unity of theology and pastoral ministry, for this unity is not yet sufficiently practiced. Liturgy and catechesis, for example, are closely related and, as ministries in a local church, are mutually enhancing. Yet, if liturgists attended to the worship event as if it were in some kind of liturgical box, unaffected by the habits of the heart and the life practices of those who worship, they would be making a systemic error. Here I approach catechesis as *a ministry to the practice* of the community's understandings, a description with implications central to this book's agenda.

This chapter questions what the local church stands for, but it does so by beginning with worship, examining what we do when we gather around the altar. As a whole this book begins and ends there, both from my own conviction and because of strategy.[2] Starting with the altar gathering is an approach designed to get at what is unquestioned in most local congregations, namely, an assumption not always articulated by many churchgoers that if verbalized in an oversimplified form would appear as "We worship; therefore, we are good; we are a godly people." I want to question that logic and inquire about the sort of transformative power liturgy possesses and the conditions under which it urges us towards transformation.

Was the Eucharist ever celebrated by those guarding the death camps in Germany, and if so, what did it mean? In the years of the 1970s and early 1980s when almost ten thousand young people were "disappeared," murdered, in Argentina, that nation's generals gathered yearly with Roman Catholic bishops to celebrate what was called the Military Mass. As far as I know, no outcry came from the living voices assembled there, but we might surmise about the cries uttered by the spirits of the dead.[3] Are there conditions of celebrating the Eucharist that effectively camouflage its connection to the lives we are currently living? This question about liturgy's power might seem to be an outmoded one, having been settled in the Reformation controversies about the efficacy of sacraments in a sinful church.[4] I wish to raise it again, however, for its implications for our understanding of what the local church is meant to be and the processes by which it becomes what it is meant to be. The issue is a pastoral and catechetical one.

More than ever, the question of ritual's transformative power brings with it further unsettling questions about the more deeply transformative, yet unrecognized, power, for good or ill, of the life structure of particular communities.[5] We claim the "enacted word" of ritual has the ability to move worshipers into the mystery being celebrated and also toward the Christian way, using powerful communicative means that transcend logic. The various sensual signs used in ritual — gesture, movement, word, sung prayer, bread and wine, water, oil, incense — all these work to bring subtle realities to vivid awareness. As a core element in the perdurance of a centuries-old tradition, ritual itself carries forward the tradition in a way doctrinal statements alone cannot. Such convictions show great confidence in the liturgy's directive and corrective power in a worshiping community.[6]

However, the actual functioning of worship is not so simple. Can ritual in certain situations function as a kind of camouflage keeping hidden and out of sight the radical questions a ritual should contain? Can the "worship event" camouflage a radical attempt to avoid the encounter with God? Can signs meant to reveal deceive? Though the correct ritual language and gestures are used, are there contexts in which they cannot signify? The Eucharist, the enacted memory of Jesus and his disciples bonded in the Spirit of God, now bonded in this community via bread and wine, has implications for how a community lives out its relatedness, its resources, and its obedience to God. Those implications can be successfully ignored or resisted. If the Eucharist becomes untethered from the community's life, no longer anchored, say, in a struggle for fidelity, a life-giving connection has been severed. While the meanings expressed in liturgical ritual remain historically embedded in a tradition, those using the ritual may not be so embedded in the tradition's understandings at all and may be much more securely embedded in the signification system of a culture having little in common with the religious tradition. Catherine Bell wisely warns of "the tendency to isolate ritual from all other forms of social activity."[7] The ritual's sacramentality cannot be isolated from wider, related forms of sacramentality.

A key question for liturgy today is whether, in light of what a particular community actually stands for, ritual is capable of being an authentic expression of the life of that community. Or put the other way around, can what a particular group actually stands for in its everyday life be of such a character that the Eucharist cannot signify it? In other words, the Eucharist would be a countersign of that life. When what the community does outside the ritual space is a countersign of the gospel, the sign value of what it does within the ritual space has little effect. Worse, the Eucharist could be a ritual lie. A principle I am using here is this: liturgical speech is self-implicating speech; to the extent it is not, it is not liturgical speech. In the United States "self-implication" has a negative tone since it is often used in connection with not admitting to involvement in evil. Those not wishing to implicate themselves by admitting wrongdoing invoke their Fifth Amendment rights. But here I am using self-implication in a very positive sense of deliberately implicating oneself in the work of Jesus, no matter what the consequences. In what activity were the Argentine generals and their cleric cohorts implicating themselves when they gathered in that cathedral, in a lilting hymn of life or a drumroll of death?

Rituals can perdure long after their significance has been lost. In the village of Dunquin in southwest Ireland, a huge pile of stones stands close to a holy well. They obviously were put there by human hand. When I asked a man who had lived most of his life near that well how the pile of stones came to be there, he said the local people every March trekked to the spot and each threw one or more stones onto the pile. He had no idea what this practice meant but thought it had been going on from ancient days. One might think that when a ritual becomes a historical curiosity, it would no longer be used to express religious meaning. True, but the process by which a ritual ceases to signify is gradual, not immediate. Sri Lankan theologian Aloysius Pieris chooses the word "fade" to get at the gradualness of this process:

> A religion fades out of history when its symbols and institutions lose their capacity to evoke among its followers the distinctive salvific experience that defines its essence. Did not this happen to the great religions of Ancient Egypt, Rome, Greece, and Mesopotamia?[8]

Notice Pieris's nuance. It is not that the ritual loses its life; after all, ritual is no more nor less than an expressive medium. What becomes defective is a relationship: the one between the ritual and the believers. Among the assembled worshipers, the "distinctive salvific experience" ceases to be compelling and thus cannot be expressed or evoked in ritual. The worshipers have ceased to implicate themselves in the ritual's words and actions. The life, understanding, and commitments of the followers are the key component in this dialectic. When a religion loses its communicative capacity for religious seekers, it eventually dies, as do the rituals that allowed it to express its religious insight. When religious seekers halt their search or come to find "salvation" in something other than God, a religion, along with its ritual media, perishes. In a sense, ritual has no meaning in itself apart from the intention of some actual person or group; when that group is totally in the past, the ritual has become a museum piece.

Vision and Intention in Worship

In this section and the following one I highlight two closely related matters: (1) the centrality of intention (a seminal form of self-implication) in any liturgical assembly and (2) the indispensable need for that intention to be actually lived by the community. Liturgiologist Geoffrey Wainwright notes that a Christian worshiping assembly, and by extension any group following a religious way, embodies a "vision" and a version of reality. His use of the word "vision" suggests a religious imagining of the possibilities of human life and of living that vision. The religious group inhabits this vision and makes it tangible to itself and accessible to others. Worship's sacramentality is dependent on the sacramentality of the life of the local ecclesial body.

> A historical community...can transmit a vision of reality which helps decisively in the interpretation of life and the world....
>
> It is the Christian community that transmits the vision which the theologian, as an individual human being, has seen and believed.... *Worship* is the place in which that vision comes to a sharp focus, a concentrated expression, and it is here that the vision has often been found to be at its most appealing.[9]

Seeing ritual as "regular patterns of behavior invested with symbolic significance and efficacy"[10] by a particular group of persons puts special emphasis on the subjectivity of the worshipers. They must find in a particular ritual, though often patterned according to ancient prescription, an authentic and meaningful way of expressing their religious vision today.

Of course, once entered with the self-implicating purpose of expressing faith, ritual embodies for a community the dimensions of faith beyond discursive speech. The worshiping group says through ritual, "This reality is something that grasps us." Ritual's self-implicating symbols may carry a group (or individuals in the group) to a grasp of religious mystery beyond words, to wonder and contemplation. Lacking that grasp or vision, these ways are as inert as museum artifacts. The underlying issue in worship is religious vision, subjectivity, and intentionality — and the practices that flow from them. Vatican Council II makes this point clear:

> In order that the sacred liturgy may produce its full effect, it is necessary that the faithful come to it with proper dispositions,

that their thoughts match their words, and that they cooperate with divine grace lest they receive it in vain. Pastors of souls must therefore realize that, when the liturgy is celebrated, more is required than the mere observance of the laws governing valid and licit celebration. It is their duty to ensure that the faithful take part knowingly, actively, and fruitfully.[11]

Neither now nor in the past has having the proper dispositions been automatic or easy.

The history of Christianity shows that concern for the proper dispositions was an intense one for early Christians. Their response was catechetical. For any person to be invited to worship, she or he had to engage first in a relatively intense period of preparation involving instruction, baby steps in new patterns of living, scrutiny of life patterns, clarification, change, further instruction, and so forth. Such preparation, called the *catechumenate*, was a period of significant change lasting up to three years. Its deep self-implication or conversion remains the norm of the church: "Before persons can come to the liturgy, they must be called to faith and to conversion."[12] Liturgical ritual does not of itself invest nonbelievers or even beginners with understanding; instead, they first come to an understanding authenticated by living and then express that vision in worship. Such was the procedure of the ancient catechumenate.

Vision and Life Structure

A vision of life is not verified so much by its truth claims as in the life practice it fosters or produces, which is why a key feature of the early procedure for preparing neophytes for full membership in the church was the correction of life practice. Understanding was not sufficient; correct practice of that understanding was an indispensable precondition. Perhaps better than we, early Christians saw the community's life as the primary sacrament of the presence of the Spirit of Jesus. That is why in the third century Origen wrote, "The profound and secret mysteries must not be given, at first, to disciples, but they must be first instructed in the correction of their life style." In another place, Origen is more explicit: "When it becomes evident that the disciples are purified and *have begun, as far as possible, to live better* [emphasis added], only then are they invited to know our mysteries."[13] In effect,

Origin was saying, "When they are deeply self-implicated in the Jesus Way, . . ." Was he also suggesting before bread and wine can be transformed into the Body and Blood of Christ, the community itself must be so transformed as a prior condition?

Regis Duffy's study of the catechumenate as the shaper of life structure emphasizes that before being admitted to the community of worshipers, the candidate had to have succeeded, beyond any merely stated desire, in transforming his or her way of life:

> One major characteristic of the catechumenal process . . . [was]: God's Word leads to commitments long before it leads to initiation. . . . Three years "hearing the word" in the catechumenate of Hippolytus at Rome might seem long until we reflect on the quality of commitment that was expected of any Christian at the time. Hippolytus tells us that the first time inquirers came "in order to hear the word," the teachers questioned them on their motivation, their life situation, and their willingness to change work that might hinder the practice of God's word.[14]

Here the ministry of the word, catechesis, functions as a ministry to practice and to the understandings needed for practice. Catechesis is the activity supporting the sacramentality of the community's life as evidence of Jesus' continued presence. Unhappily, the implications of the early communities' preoccupation with life practice have not been sufficiently applied to worship today. If we accept that worship is no "pure" realm of activity independent of the lived vision of the worshipers and if we further accept that the actual vision of life brought to worship is influenced by the pattern of commitment worked out in one's life practice, then the everyday life practices of both individuals and of the local church itself need examination.

That the way of worship is also the way of believing has come to be widely accepted, as in the formula *lex orandi, lex credendi*. This formula needs, if not a corrective, then at least an addendum, to avoid liturgical overstatement. My addendum would be the formula *lex vivendi, lex credendi*, or even *lex vivendi, lex orandi*.[15] The way we live determines what we actually believe; what directs our life determines our prayer. Our way of living has religious consequences. This is a long-standing principle of spirituality, and it is true for communities and families as well as individuals.

As life structure goes,[16] so go the *enacted* beliefs of the community. The quality of the community's worship is determined more by the quality of the community's life structure, that is, actual patterns of living, than by the quality of the words spoken or the rituals enacted during worship. Put more simply: the sacramentality of worship and the sacramentality of life practice cannot be divorced. These sacramentalities must whisper to each other. As a ministry to the practice of communal understanding, catechesis is an indispensable requirement for the nurture of worship. For a credible Christian life, the proper relationship among all three elements — life structure, worship, and belief — is crucial. The position of philosopher C. S. Peirce demonstrates his recognition of this relationship:

> Belief consists mainly in being deliberately prepared to adopt the formula believed in as the guide to action; the essence of belief is the establishment of a habit; and different beliefs are distinguished by the different modes of action to which they give rise.[17]

Writing about Christian life at the end of the second century, Thomas Finn notes the same idea: "[T]he cardinal principle that permeated early catechetics was that any belief not embodied in conduct was not true belief."[18] Lacking behavior consonant with the belief, one has grounds for doubting whether there is in fact a belief.

Life structure is becoming progressively more important as a religious issue, possibly because of the new ways life structure is being socially and culturally shaped. Jacques Ellul, for example, points out that a concern for the actual practice of truth is something Christians and Marxists have in common:

> In one respect there is...an obvious point of similarity between what takes place in Marxism and in Christianity. Both have made practice the touchstone of truth or authenticity. In other words, it is by practice that we have to appreciate or not the intentions or purity of the doctrine, of the truth of the origin or source. The link between praxis and theory in Marx is well known. One should not forget, however, that it is a circular link. This means finally that false practice inevitably engenders false theory, and one can see the falsity of practice not only from its effects...but also by the new theory to which it gives birth....Christianity too, judges itself by practice. We thus confront a constant challenge in this regard.[19]

The Problem of Practice

If we accept that the material conditions of our life create the mindset and perceptions that direct our lives, we may be as close to the convictions of the early Christians as to those of Marx. These conditions provide the interpretive context facilitating or debilitating our response to God's call. The choices we make and follow become our embodied commitments, and they include our choice of work, of residence, of mode of transportation, of friends, of patterns of eating and interacting with family and friends, of our way of using finances, of our way of getting information about the world we live in, and of our use of leisure time. Note that all these matters are for us choices that then become structures in our life pattern. These choices-become-patterns-of-action shape our consciousness, our values and biases about the world, our concerns. Whenever we walk into a place of worship, these patterned commitments walk in with us. The frightening thing about the Military Mass in Buenos Aires was, not the ornamental dress — ecclesiastical or military — that walked into that cathedral, but the attitudes and lifeways that walked in with both the presiding and nonpresiding celebrants. Whatever word or hymn of praise we utter has our attitudes and lifeways as its horizon. This matter is generally overlooked in current literature on worship and spirituality.

As ritual is a patterned way of expressing, so life structure is a patterned way of acting. These two patterned ways are either coherent or incoherent one to the other. Those whose life structure is alien to the gospel may come to the ritual and join in speaking its patterned responses, but these belie, and not necessarily in the awareness of the "worshipers," the lived commitments. One could say that worship should be a zone of contestation that puts to those gathered the question of credibility regarding their lived commitments — but it is such a zone only if the worshipers are in search of greater credibility and coherence in their faith lives. Unfortunately, the pattern of expression in ritual and the way ritual itself is conceptualized may overlook the connections between lived commitments and ritual affirmations. Ritual affirmations may be smooth and easy, their casual character disguising their inability to engage the mind and heart. On the other hand, the pattern of acting in life structure tends to be stubborn and more inexorable than casual.

Not many years ago, I traveled to Texas to facilitate a four-day retreat for a group of ministers, all from the same denomination, held at a camp in a rural area. Having arrived Saturday evening in a major city to await Sunday-afternoon transportation to the retreat, I went to Sunday worship at one of the denomination's churches, at the edge of one of its large universities. The service was attended by fashionably dressed upper-class adults, with no teens and almost no one in their twenties present. In a city of serious racial tensions, the worshipers were all Caucasian, though there were two blacks in the choir, which was of such sophistication it may have been salaried. I thought to myself: here we have the elite of this city, those who make it run and whose decisions influence the lives of the general populace, and I am with them at worship, the activity that puts God at the center of reality. As the service unfolded, I became aware that nothing we did during that hour gave attention to any specific matter in the lives of the assembled, in the city and region or in the state or in the country. It was totally out of this world. All was effectively contained by the church walls and so unfocused it seemed only marginally religious. If anything, the pace and flow of the service implicitly affirmed the persons assembled, their habits of control, their sense of being in charge. Nothing was questioned, but then nobody but the preacher spoke. I was hesitant in these judgments. I had come to pray not to judge, and I suspected my own reactions as jaundiced. At the retreat, whose main theme was "discipleship and culture," I intended to say nothing of my visit to this church, fearing to offend my fellow retreatants. However, as our interaction on discipleship and culture evolved, it seemed appropriate to tell of my Sunday worship and hesitant reflections. The group understood all too well and explained the gender, racial, and class divisions within their denomination.

My theoretical contrast here between what is said and done in the zone of ritual and what is lived in the zone of everyday living seeks to expose a problem needing more attention. I accept that worshipers serious about the call to discipleship and its behavioral implications do not engage in worship casually. Ritual puts them in a struggle for coherence between the pattern of ritual worship and the pattern of life structure, and that struggle is never casual. It is fully self-implicating. My claim is that ritual's connection to life practice has for too long been taken for granted. One could easily compile a long bibliography of writings before and after Vatican II about the aesthetics of enactment in ritual: the dignified and orchestrated enactment in the beautifully proportioned space. Unfortunately, not much reflection has been done on worship's connection to the aesthetics of life practice, which is a *moral category* preoccupied with the beauty of a life centered in the Lord Jesus and seeking to follow his commitments. Liturgy as aesthetics is a sham if not bonded to the loveliness of a life of struggle for fidelity.

The situation of Christians today in many parts of the world underscores the importance of the struggle for greater coherence between worship and life structure. When the Roman Catholics from the wealthy elite families in Guatemala attend the Eucharist, they say the same words in the same ritual as those whose friends and relatives were killed by the death squads for announcing the good news of justice. One can attend a Eucharist while never engaging in "communio," in the sense of being connected in the Spirit of Jesus with one's sisters and brothers. The Gospels question the fake "communio," which names as fellows those of similar economic condition, social class, race, sex, or sexual orientation. Mark Searle reminds us that "as liturgical reforms were introduced there was a great deal of pulpit rhetoric about 'building community,' but too little appreciation...that the community (or better 'communion') is something already given in baptism, i.e., that already existing communion in Christ and the Spirit...which continually seeks adequate expression in the structures and lifestyle of the local community."[20] In the case of the two groups of worshipers in Guatemala, the same ritual is not being invested with the same meaning. Because of such situations, this matter of life structure and practice calls for more attention and study, and two modern thinkers — Raymond Williams and Pierre Bourdieu — have offered helpful understanding of the ways life structure is shaped.

Social Influences on Life Structure

Raymond Williams claimed in a lifetime of writing that one could understand society through studying its forms of communication. The means of communication are a key part of the material conditions of a society's life, which ultimately shape consciousness.[21] Begun in the twentieth century a communications revolution is still underway, and its power to shape the way we perceive and what we value is still not adequately assessed. Film and television, with their penchant for narrative, offer vivid imaginations of the purpose and possibilities of the human project. And those who imagine the meaning of life for others hold great power in those others' lives. The power of such narratives cannot be appreciated until we recognize how tightly bound they are to consumer capitalism and the production of consumption. Advertising's strategic use of a persistent image tied to a persistent slogan shapes the consciousness of even those who think they resist. Advertising has perfected in this century the orchestration of desire as the foundation of its production of consumption. Person becomes defined as consumer, perhaps not in formal definition but more in one's basic assumptions, in patterns of purchasing, and in modes of possession.

Intense religious issues are at stake here. Consumerism is a religion promising salvation through the wisdom of the right purchase and with goods as its sacramental signs. Would it not be ironic for advertisers to give their astute attention to behavior while religion to all effects ignores behavior? When worshipers who have ingested the religion of consumerism bring it unnamed and unrecognized into the place of worship, we have a radical conflict between two claims of ultimacy, the overt one of a formal religion and the covert one of the consumerist faith. The conflict and the issues at stake in it have been expressed well by John Kavanaugh:

> The great paradox of finding one's identity in wealth is ultimately the paradox of all idolatries: entrusting ourselves to our products, our silver and golden gods, *we become fashioned — re-created — in their image and likeness.* Bereft of personhood and human sensibility, we lose our vision. We become voiceless, unable to utter words of life and love.... To make wealth one's god is to become brittle and cold, to become like unto a thing, to become invulnerable, impenetrable, unloving.[22]

Embracing a religion involves embracing the vision of human life proposed by its gods, be it the God of life or the god of "stuff." When a community enters worship in touch with the message of Jesus and its deep contestation of the consumer ethos, the act of worship celebrates the gospel in a way that itself radically contests that ethos.

While Raymond Williams shows how communications structures influence thought and ultimately action, French sociologist Pierre Bourdieu's concern is with the relation of social structure and action. Bourdieu claims that economies produce in people the dispositions demanded by the economy and by the position people have in that economy.[23] To a religiously committed person this claim at first appears startling since it says something about the shaping of a person's spirit, here termed "dispositions." Bourdieu is talking about the shaping of a spirituality. Religious persons, preferring to think that religious values shape one's dispositions, might resist Bourdieu's position. Indeed the cogency of his claim only gradually emerges from the data that under-gird his theory. (For consideration of Bourdieu's ideas in more detail, see chapter 5, which deals with the formative power of life structure.)

What Bourdieu invites us to ponder is not the condition of religious understanding but the condition of life practice that exists along with, and sometimes belies, religious understanding. Robert Coles and George Abbott White have almost intuited Bourdieu's insight in the following description of worship in the churches of the well-to-do:

> There is more order [in the churches of the rich than in those of the poor], but order of a different kind, more self-regard in the way in which one worships. Attention is paid, and in a certain way: to what one sees and what one hears and what one reads, yes, but also, significantly, to oneself. You enter the churches of the privileged full of yourself. You are well-dressed, pleased to be in a place where you are treated well, with great respect and personal attention, and where there will be — and this is impor-tant — no surprises. The format is fixed and the words and music are modulated, no extremes either from church or from those who are at worship. Without having been told, you understand that if anything happens to you of a spiritual nature, you are to keep it to yourself. Just as there are certain words used in certain ways in rural services, these privileged places of worship have theirs and time moves along here in a measured (but pleasant) fashion.

> By contrast [with the worship of the poor] there are no un-planned stops at this word, no responses or outbreaks to that moment of sound; in these places of worship there are no abrupt moves forward or doubling back, either in response to the minis-ter or those at worship. As I said, the privileged ones do not like to be surprised; they have not come to be confronted or to be put into situations where they are not in control.[24]

Of course there is another side to this matter, to which the passage al-ludes. The kind of ecstatic stirrings, the eruptions of the Word among the worshipers, the uncontainable grief and joy found in the churches of the poor, show other possibilities — creatively disruptive ones — of wor-ship. Social class influences the ways of the liturgical assembly. Aloysius Pieris pointed this out in his extraordinary claim that "no religious persecution under a Marxist regime can be compared to the under-mining of religious values which capitalist technocracy generates in our cultures.... The latter pollutes religion by betraying it to Mammon."[25]

The Role of Catechesis/Christian Education

The preoccupation of catechesis is not so much the condition of the community's understanding of the Christian message as *the condition of the community's practice of that understanding.* Pieris has noted how early in Christianity, especially in Irenaeus's writings, there was a shift in emphasis from discipleship being primarily a way of acting to being a way of understanding. According to Pieris, it was the monastic movement, strongly influenced by non-Christian monastic movements, that in its move to the desert or to enclaves of rigorous practice maintained the early emphasis on Christianity as an art of living.[26] In highlighting the persistent attempts of the church to find the correct lived way, Pieris never underestimates — and neither should we — the difficulties of finding and living that way. We do well to avoid naive claims, such as G. A. Coe's, made earlier this century, that religious education could foster a revolution in U.S. society at large. Still I believe that local churches can be, though not easily, zones of contestation of the class-based patterns and of the dominant culture.

One of the reasons I have in my own studies gone back again and again to C. Ellis Nelson's *Where Faith Begins* is for its emphasis on the connection between the faith understood and the faith lived. Other works have claimed to be concerned about practice, though few exhibit the focused concern for the lived way that Nelson's does. His convictions behind the book are close to my own. In Nelson's words,

> It is an assumption of this book that America is increasingly becoming a secular, pluralistic, urban society and that the Protestant ethos which dominated when the Constitution was written is no longer the ethos of the country generally. It is further assumed that the Christian faith is based on a revelation from God which transcends culture and comes into human life for the purpose of directing human culture. It is essential, therefore, that we explore what culture communicates in order to separate *to some extent* [emphasis his] the Christian tradition from culture.[27]

Nelson's concern consistently is with the worshiping, believing community as the zone where the Christian tradition lives to some extent separated from the wider culture. Though he does not use this exact language, Nelson's intent is to propose the local church as a zone of cultural contestation. In the members' living faithful practice one finds the most cogent and coherent expression of what that faith means for our time.

Nelson's and my own intent will be seriously misunderstood unless readers see we are both open to and affirming of the world. We both hold that Christians are called to be basically friendly toward the world at the same time their very love of its possibilities allows them to bring all facets of the world to religious judgment. My love for a friend and hers for me does not mean we affirm everything each other does. On the contrary our love means we see each other's actions in the light of his or her special qualities and possibilities. Should she see me seeming to betray my basic stance, her very friendliness toward me might prompt her to intervene with a word of caution. She does not condemn; instead she says in effect, "I sense here a crisis between the true you and the lesser you. I speak because I care."[28] If I hear only hostility in what she says, I will not be able to listen to her caution. To listen, I must see her basic stance of friendliness. The comparison of "the world," a mental construct, to a friend, who is a particular living being, is imperfect but still useful. One can judge the world from a religious stance that is lovingly judgmental, out of a richer imagination of what human life is all about. Readers will have to decide from the following pages if my intent seems basically world-friendly, as I claim, or unfriendly. The world needs the loving contestation of religious groups who have reimagined the possibilities of the human along the lines of their sacred texts.

Nelson sees a gift to the world in religious particularity, embraced by particular groups for themselves. In a passage I have often cited, Nelson expresses this conviction in a compelling way:

> After seeing that the group of believers is the unity with which we must work, we must then see that whatever is done or said, or not done or not said, is teaching. There is no such thing as postponing the solution to a problem. The decision to postpone is a decision; it teaches that the issue is too hot to handle, that such issues are not appropriate for the church, or that the tactic of postponement is more important at this point than a resolution to settle the matter. People learn from the way events are handled. There is no neutrality. If a congregation attempts to be neutral, it teaches that on the issues at hand it can't make up its mind, it is fearful of the result of a decision, or it is confused about how to proceed. There is no avoidance of an issue. Not to see an issue is to teach

that Christians do not see issues. Christians who avoid problems in social ethics — such as involvement in racial relations, war, or the distribution of wealth — are saying that the Christian faith does not operate in these areas.... What the congregation as a group says and does in the community is the meaning they give to their faith.[29]

From this view, Christian education, or catechesis, is a ministry to the condition of the community's practice of its understandings. In this view, also, the community is to be in some sense a school of practice, not of practice imposed on those too young to resist but of practice sought after by those who seek to be disciples. If the community is to be a zone of contestation, then its members can together discover how to embody the contesting values in their life structure. Congregations adept at setting up schools of doctrine, to ensure a proper understanding of its tenets, can also become schools of practice, with a ministry to practice.

Competence in the living practice of discipleship is learned in situations. Like language, it is learned, inextricably, as the mastery of practice but also as the practical mastery of situations, in which one becomes able to act in a way adequate to the gospel. Discipleship is not a "thought" art but a lived-out one. The churches' interest in the verbal mastery of doctrinal tenets and in the spoken language of discipleship has generally not been matched by adequate attention to the living practice of fidelity, except perhaps in matters of sexual morality. As one form of practice having to do with gospel values, ritual behavior in worship is not sufficient to show a full range of competence. Competence in discipleship must also, and characteristically, exhibit competent practice in a variety of situations.[30] Viewed as competence, discipleship enters no pure, unsullied realm of perfect competence. Competence is a relative category; a person or a group struggles to refine practice constantly. Lacking that struggle for greater competence, any competence withers like the fig tree of the Gospels.

Achieving this competence over a period of time is difficult. It is much easier to idealize who we are and what we are, honoring a fantasy, while overlooking the actuality of who we are. The result is a painful distance between what we intone in our worship and what we inscribe in our lives. What we live we dare not name, and what we name we dare not live.

The Problem of Stance

There is a need here to deal with the large question of religious vision. Which one are we talking about? In the religious climate of the United States, Christians are aware that they do not all espouse the same faith. They claim the same sacred writings, but they apply their writings in very different ways, with different implications for the political and economic orders. In a country of perhaps 4 percent of the world's population holding the rest of the world hostage to its globally destructive economic order, some Christians seek to find a stance that will radically contest the dominant culture. My own view is that in a consumerist culture no gospel stance so radically contests the dominant ethos as does solidarity with the poor. Similar stances might include solidarity with victims and bonding with the disenfranchised. Such stances load Christianity with important economic and political agendas that have deep implications for life structure and practice in local communities. Perhaps the difficulty of actually taking such stances verifies Bourdieu's claims about the priority of economic status in fostering habits of the heart and of action. In the context of lived-out commitments to the poor and victims, worship becomes a coherent celebration of dangerous memories. Lacking them, worship becomes, if not an actual celebration of class privilege, then a celebration of its being overlooked and ignored.

Questions for Discussion and Reflection

1. Do the pastoral leaders you know adequately maintain the connections between the gospel and what the people are actually living in their everyday lives? To what extent does the theology you read shed light on pastoral reality?

2. How helpful is it to name catechesis or Christian education as a ministry to the community's *practice* of its understanding, rather than as a ministry to its understanding? What difference does it make in practical terms?

3. Can you think of any examples of worship disguising or camouflaging the true character of a congregation's life? Are there conditions under which worship is authentic? Inauthentic? What are such conditions?

4. One formula found in the chapter is "The way we live our lives is the way we pray and the way we believe." In what ways might

this proposition be helpful? Are there any dangers in it? What steps can pastoral guides take toward better preparation of a congregation's dispositions for worship?

5. The author claims that the choices we make eventually structure our lives and our way of thinking. What is the significance of this idea for the local church? Can you extend the writer's thinking by offering more examples of how life structure does in fact influence our attitudes and dispositions?

6. "Liturgy as aesthetics is a sham if not bonded to the loveliness of a life of struggle for fidelity." How helpful is such a statement? Might it lead to "pulpit moralizing" that is unhelpful to anyone? Are there ways it might lead to better focused and more honest worship?

7. Do you believe consumerism is a kind of religion that walks into the worship space with members of the congregation? Do you believe that Christian assemblies should be or could be "zones of contestation" of the wider culture, particularly its consumerism?

CHAPTER TWO

THE MATERIAL CONDITIONS OF OUR SEEING AND PERCEIVING

Religious Implications of the Power of Images

THROUGHOUT THIS BOOK, I seek to describe the situation of the local church while also offering, not formulas, but ways of thinking about how we might become a congregation struggling for fidelity. The concern regarding worship extends to examining how the symbols, images, and meanings of our religious heritage are overshadowed and even drowned out by the powerful electronic communications media now evolving exponentially every decade. How can religious commitments be maintained in religious congregations in the face of the wider society's ability to press its messages on us incessantly? Put another way, how can a religious stance be maintained in the face of the new era of electronic communications? The question is a crucial one for local congregations.[1] How do Christians maintain Jesus' imagination of the human in the time of an electronically communicated imagination of the person as the one who dominates and then consumes? In this chapter I will be dealing with shifts in the imagination, including the imagination of religious people.

Images and the Imagination

Concern for how we imagine is not new. We find it in the Jewish refusal to tolerate graven images and penchant for paradox as a way of insisting things are not what they seem. In the Christian tradition, a consistent body of literature has dealt with controlling the imagination as a way of restructuring practice. We find concern for the imagination in the zany metaphors and images of Paul and later in the highly symbolic tales of the Desert Fathers and Mothers. In the sixteenth century, Ignatius Loyola's Spiritual Exercises, and the centuries of systematic writing on spirituality that followed it, gave special attention to the role of imagination in distorting or directing religious commitments. Of course, this tradition is founded in Jesus' own parables and paradoxical sayings that stick in one's head because they bring forward puzzling and haunting questions that reimagine the purposes of human life. In his Christmas oratorio, *For the Time Being*, W. H. Auden reminds us that Jesus redeems the human imagination from imaginative promiscuity: "[I]n Him the Flesh is united to the Word without magical transformation; imagination is redeemed from promiscuous fornication with her own images."[2] What after all is the meaning of gathering around an altar, calling on the one Jesus named Father, remembering and thanking, breaking bread and sharing a common cup as signs of oneness, all the while cherishing God's gifts — if it is not a dramatic imaginative refocusing?

The problem of the human imagination is a special one in our time, when we all have access to an endless stream of graphic, acted-out narratives, all implicitly telling us, This is what life is all about. How can we resist messages we receive unawares? Could it happen that secular commentators offer more caution about images and seeing than religious people offer?

I have come to see that no major issue affecting us today can be properly approached without attention to how that issue affects the imagination. Students walk into my university marriage class with their imaginations already captivated by images and filmed narratives depicting human gender relations. Within the same day they may excitedly accept a written critique of gender relations but later ingest without question an imaged depiction of those same relations directly contradicting the written critique. Adept at the written word, they may overlook the implications of the graphic depiction. My first step is to try to bring to light these ways of imagining relationships — and question them. Reimagining is a crucial but difficult educational task. It is a significant, largely overlooked pastoral issue.

Images, so easily taken for granted, have an importance in the human enterprise that cannot be overstated. Am I suggesting that the new electronically communicated culture is inherently bad? No. Neither is the strange dog I must get past to be on my way. I approach the dog with a cautious friendliness until I judge it is not dangerous; then I may even pet it. The electronically communicated culture needs to be examined and thought about regarding its implications for religious persons. The situation needs to be judged.[3] George Gerbner's alarming conviction that the stories children once heard mostly told by parents are now mostly told by TV has religious implications. Of course not just the stories told in homes but the homes themselves, their shape and configuration, have been shifted to accommodate media. Domestic space has been transformed by being designed around "walls of (moving) images," as the domestic space of the media. To be in this private domestic space transformed by media technology is to be able to see, to be an onlooker of, presumably the whole world.[4] Here we find disrupted the previous boundaries between night and day, depth and surface, here and there, home and exterior or street. Space is detached from place. Again, this shift is in itself neither good nor bad — but it needs to be judged.

Because of the visual side of the electronic communications revolution, most people today are awash in a sea of images affecting their sense of reality, even as they cease to pay them explicit attention. The material conditions of our seeing — what we see, the contexts in which we see, the frequency of our seeing, the volume of the images that come tumbling out of our TV and movie screens, as well as from the printed pages we scan — these conditions are not innocent and ought not be overlooked, though generally they are. They are the wider social conditions under which any worshiping group actually lives and assembles for liturgy. These conditions affect us and our religious dispositions. How do images work in society, and how do they influence us? What are the religious implications?

My purpose is to increase awareness of the dilemmas of religious people in "the time of the sign." Because the conditions of our seeing have so much influence on our perceptions, these conditions represent a special task for educators, pastoral guides, and all others concerned about religious ways of seeing. Pastoral workers aware of the images used in their own tradition are marginally aware, at best, of the wider array of images most people take in every day and of the possible and effective ways these counter or negate the images of the religious tradition.[5] Everyday images tend to be outside of any religious discourse. In what ways may the images we encounter when we gather around the altar be in conflict with the images we encounter when we gather around the tube? Can we attend to the significance of this conflict? To address such questions, I will move through two treatments of images, the first dealing with the power of images and seeking to recover a new alertness to the fact of that power. The second examines how images influence our perception and behavior.

Freedberg's Study of Responses to the Power of Images

In David Freedberg's study of the power of images in history, his approach to the functioning of images has a particular genius.[6] He does not analyze specific images so much as accounts how various persons responded to images, as far back as Greco-Roman times. His basic method is found in the title and subtitle of his provocative book *The Power of Images: Studies in the History and Theory of Response*. Freedberg's study of these responses discloses a range of ways visual images have affected people's emotions and perceptions. Tears, affection, anger, sexual desire, contemplative ecstasy, arduous journeys, and even violent revolt have all been stimulated by pictures and sculpture, down to the present. While many today acknowledge the historical evidence of these past responses, we tend to deny such responses are possible to us in the present. We are convinced images do not affect us: "We repress the evidence of responses clearly revealed by past behavior because we are too embarrassed by it, and... because we fear the strength of the effects of images on ourselves."[7] Freedberg sees some of the abstruse discourse about the formal qualities of images as analytic strategies for gaining conceptual control over the power we fear in images. In a time when evidence of the influence of images on contemporary behavior abounds, his book offers a needed acknowledgment of the power latent in various kinds of visual images.

Freedberg offers apt examples of this power down through the ages. In a third-century romance by Heliodorus, an Ethiopian queen provides the explanation for her daughter's being born with white skin so uncommon in her country: during intercourse, the mother had looked upon the picture of naked, white-skinned Andromeda adorning her bedchamber "and so by mishap engendered presently a thing like to her."[8] While to us this view represents a new genetic dimension of image erotics, the queen's "unscientific" view of the potency of images had in fact persisted through the Middle Ages, with vestiges lingering even to our own day, despite our purported immunity to images. Freedberg cites Augustine's account, based on the medical writer Soranus, of the badly deformed ruler Dionysius. This tyrant was in such fear of producing children like himself that he placed before his wife a picture of a handsome male, which might stimulate her desire and thereby transmit its beauty to the offspring she might conceive. Such convictions about images continued through the Renaissance and beyond to the

Counter-Reformation, where their power is affirmed, even if negatively, by exhortations to remove from bedchambers all pictures other than those of one's spouse because of their dangerous physical and moral ramifications.

Long after Augustine, pictures were placed in the nursery and household for their influence on the upbringing of children. Freedberg brings forward Dominici's 1403 *Rule for the Management of Family Care*, in which the fifteenth-century writer lists twenty-two different kinds of edifying pictures and sculptures that "would give them [children] love of virginity with their mother's milk, desire for Christ, hatred of sins, disgust at vanity, shrinking from bad companions, and a beginning through considering the saints, of contemplating the supreme Saint of saints."[9] For Dominici, the effectiveness of such images comes from the identification of the child with those in the pictures and from the delight the child takes in persons that are "like himself." For the children, such images were mirrors. This account could trigger reflection on the apathy many contemporary parents show toward the images their children of various ages ingest in their formative years. Freedberg, however, elects to stay with Dominici's evident claim that images have effective potential to affect children, not just emotionally but with consequences for long-term behavior. Images have influence in people's lives, including the lives of little people. What do modern commentators make of such a claim? As quoted by Freedberg, one commentator wrote that Dominici "did not rank painting very high, considering it useful for small children's religious education." Freedberg's response highlights the commentator's disregard of the whole question of influence: "We may well ask ourselves on just what basis the commentator *would* have Dominici rank pictures high?"[10] Those with homes wired for cable TV might ask similar questions.

Freedberg uncovers compelling evidence of the power images once were assumed to have and, at least according to eyewitness accounts, actually did have. One of these was the practice of holding before the face of someone condemned to die holy images, most often depictions of the sufferings and death of Jesus or of saints. This practice meant to ensure the condemned one would have right up to the moment of death the comfort of these images. Citing a moving sixteenth-century account of how one condemned man was moved to pray aloud and put himself in the hands of God, Freedberg asks a series of questions that become a refrain throughout his book:

Could an image really do all this, could it be that affecting and so consoling? Perhaps it is all in the report. One might feel, reading that [the condemned man] was unusually courageous and sto-ical in the face of death, that he was clearly an educated and quite learned man; and that the eyewitness may somehow have wished to glamorize his end. But this is not the point. The ques-tion is this: Why was it felt that images rather than just words could serve such a function, that they could in any way be effec-tive under such conditions? For the condemned man they may or may not have achieved their supposed purpose, but the institu-tion as a whole [of providing the condemned with such images] was based on a judgement about the efficacy of images that was predicated upon a belief in their inevitable power. And that so-cial belief cannot merely be regarded as ostensible; it appears to reflect a cognitive reality.[11]

Our current tendency to deny this power is vividly seen in art criticism of pictures with erotic content, such as the many sixteenth-century Venuses, painted with the evident sensuality of a reclining naked young woman looking directly into the eyes of her beholder. Most contem-porary criticism refuses to deal with the erotic content, replacing it with "dense iconographic readings and sensitively aesthetic evaluation of form, colors, handling and composition,"[12] which tend to repress the emotions evoked by these paintings. Schooled in such aesthetic criti-cism, we find ourselves in picture galleries unable to get in touch with basic aspects of our own reaction, including any evoking of appetite in ourselves.

As one might expect, Freedberg gives a good bit of attention to re-ligious images and their power to heal, to comfort, to call for change of behavior, and to banish evil. An anecdote allows him to highlight both the power of holy images and our own resistance to admitting their power. A colleague makes a long and difficult trip to an obscure part of France to see an ancient statue of the Virgin venerated by the devout for many centuries. Not devout herself, the colleague wants to see what made this image so famous. After forcing her way through the crowds milling in the little chapel where the statue stands, she finds a rather ugly little figure of little aesthetic interest. On her return she says to Freedberg, "I could not believe it. After so long a journey, all I saw was an ugly Madonna, with a supercilious look on her face. I was so angry with her."[13] What Freedberg finds so telling in this response is her unwitting personalization of the statue in the very breath of denying its power. The woman is not angry with an "it," that is, with the statue, but with "her," with the presence that imbues the representation, the sign becoming the living embodiment of what it signifies. Unintentionally but truly she aligns herself with those devotees who accept the presence of the "her" in the icon, thus exposing the very power she claimed to deny.

Freedberg catalogues one category of holy images in particular — those that seemed to come alive, giving rise to visions where pictures and statues speak and move. For example, the figure of Christ was said to have come down from the cross and embraced various saints, the most famous of which was Francis of Assisi, or the Virgin was claimed to have handed the Christ Child over to the hands of some favored devotee. These and similar occurrences are found represented in paintings of various centuries and in much older illuminated manuscripts. Scanning African, ancient Greek, and Christian holy images, Freedberg examines a broad range of testimonials to the power of these images. This sort of iconographic archeology is safe because it deals with past ages and extinct nations. Freedberg reminds us, however, that in our own day one would not have to travel far to find current examples of religious images evoking powerful responses from our own contemporaries or even purported to show signs of life, as in Madonnas that weep. Not surprisingly, right back to ancient times such responses have been satirized and mocked by writers as stupidity or childish illusion. We ourselves may have something to learn, not so much from the mocking satire as from the persistence of respectful, even awed, responses.

It is important to note here that Freedberg does not consider psychological aspects of the phenomena he recovers from his historical research. He is not interested in either the possible ecstatic or hysterical aspects of these responses. Rather he focuses our attention on the significance of the claimed power itself and on the fact of the observable responses to the images. In doing so, he recovers something about images we today have lost.

A vivid, secular confirmation of Freedberg's claims appeared in a *New Yorker* column recounting an event in Moscow during the dissolution of the Soviet Republic.[14] This account reflects on the TV images, broadcast by CNN hours after the Russian Republic declared its independence, of Muscovites pulling down the statue of Feliks Dzerzhinsky, former head of the KGB. One of the first spontaneous acts that independence day was for a small group of men to attack this gigantic granite statue cast in heroic pose and to try by bare-handed brute strength to topple it from its stand outside KGB headquarters. The men put a rope around its neck and strained mightily to topple it. At least while the CNN cameras were focused on their efforts, they were unsuccessful. Whether the Muscovites ultimately succeeded or not, the significance of the act — a priority for those who attempted it while ignoring the many KGB agents still roaming the streets undisturbed — points to the importance of icons of heroes and whether we accept or reject them. Of all the things these men could have done to celebrate independence, the first and most significant one chosen was to attack the icon. The power of the KGB was somehow so identified with the icon that it had to come down, as a decisive sign of the diminished power behind it.

My own interest in Freedberg's study has to do with the functioning of images today. In our time we are immersed in images but tend to deny they have any power over us, including the power to desensitize us to important human matters — to blunt our sensitivities as persons. Among the many valuable features of his analysis, the one I highlight here is its cautionary undertone, encouraging us to recognize or at least rethink both the fact of iconography and our assumption that the images we see do not affect us. If it is true that religious images influence religious people, we must at least consider the possibility that all images influence, including consumerist and violent images. The material conditions of our seeing influence the material conditions of our living.

Illusion of the Untouched Observer

In her 1985 study *Image as Insight: Visual Understanding in Western Christianity and Secular Culture*, Margaret Miles puts forth the conviction that perhaps people of past ages can offer us helpful perspectives on the functioning of images.[15] Because of the daily, continuous, and ordinary way medieval people encountered *religious* images, Miles believes their experience is close to the way contemporary people encounter media images, much closer than, say, a contemporary person's meeting of medieval images in an art museum. Still the differences remain significant, particularly the way each group would understand what happens when an object is viewed or seen. Concentrating on the physiological mechanics of seeing, modern theories of vision tend to ignore the psychological, moral, or spiritual aspects of visual encounters. Even sociological studies take a mechanistic approach in their generally unsuccessful attempt to find a causal link between, for example, media violence and the behavior of young people. In Miles's view none of our contemporary approaches deals adequately with the power of physical vision to influence the psyche. Despite our continual immersion in both commercial and entertainment images, we think of ourselves as "disengaged voyeurs." We can look, but we pretend what we see does not touch us. Medieval people had a quite different understanding of the way images worked.

As an example of the medieval understanding, Miles cites Augustine's theory of vision as a fire that animates and warms the body but has a special intensity behind the eyes. For Augustine, vision is a ray projected to focus on the object thereby forming a two-way channel which allows the object to return through the eye to be bonded to the soul and memory. Such a theory obviously takes the power of images very seriously, giving them a special efficacy in any person's life. Miles explains as follows:

> This strong visual experience was formulated negatively as the fear of contamination by a dangerous or "unsightly" visual object or positively as belief in the miraculous power of an icon, when assiduously gazed upon, to heal one's disease. Popular beliefs and practices support the conclusion that medieval people considered visual experience particularly powerful for one's good or ill. The persistence of belief in the "evil eye" from classical times to the sixteenth century and beyond is a good example. The evil eye was thought of as a maleficent visual ray of lethal strength. A person who had the evil eye reportedly could touch and poison the soul or body of an enemy. The only protections against the evil eye were making the sign of the cross, keeping one's body thoroughly covered against the baleful touch, and, especially, never meeting the eye of such a person; to do so would be to connect the two visual rays and allow the evil ray direct access to one's soul.[16]

Once prone to scoff at the concepts put forward in a university course entitled "Thomistic Psychology," I confess to finding insight in this rendition of fifth-century physiology and psychology. Whatever the exaggerations of such an understanding, its value is as a corrective to the overly mechanistic and self-deceiving contemporary view of ourselves as unaffected by what we see.[17] I have come slowly to the conviction that all images have power, in some cases obvious power but in most cases subtle, implicit power that has the special force of being unnoticed. Images and ways of imagining can subvert a religious consciousness, erode its core the way termites can eat away at the core of wood hard enough to defy a saw. We are all engaged in a "practice of seeing" almost totally overlooked.

Images and the Production of Dominative Exploitation

David Freedberg and Margaret Miles are not alone in their belief in the power of images. Their views are corroborated in the analysis of images done by the feminist lawyer Catharine MacKinnon. MacKinnon's concerns are not those of Freedberg's aesthetic critique of art nor of Miles's desire to recover the Christian tradition's varied historical "ways" of spirituality. Hers arise from alarm about the sexual brutalization and exploitation of women by means of pornography. Though ways of seeing tend to be overlooked, MacKinnon stares intently at the images and their consequences. This means that here we will have to enter a world of discourse and a range of issues different from those we have been dealing with thus far; however, the underlying issue in my presentation remains the same: the power of images in a time of images.

A fundamental point in MacKinnon's analysis is a persistent examination of the connection in our society between power and the production of images: "[P]ower constructs the appearance of reality by silencing the voices of the powerless, by excluding them from access to authoritative discourse."[18] Images are produced that depict women not just as less than men but as being brutalized or sexually assaulted. Such images are defended by many as the expression of free speech, even though in the process they erode the actual freedoms of women to be persons in the world. In the name of freedom of speech, women are denied equal protection under the law, thus allowing women to be imagined graphically as objects of exploitation.

Some find MacKinnon's claims to be extravagant, and to be sure, they have generated intense controversy, in a way verifying Freedberg's claims about both the power of images and our wish to deny that power even when starkly laid out for us by those like MacKinnon. I find her passionate eloquence about the evils of dehumanizing representations compelling and her overall argument convincing, though difficult issues like censorship are not easily resolved. The cogency of her claims becomes clearer if one accepts her fundamental conviction: Images construct reality; they define how things are. Pornography defines a woman in pornographic terms: as unequal, as a plaything for men, as one whose domination and exploitation are legally found to be neutral. This definition ultimately gives permission to men to treat women according to the definition. The condition of the way women are imaged becomes the condition of the way women are treated. Though not unrelated to Miles's and Freedberg's work on images, these claims about the power of images are new and probing.

When so many objections to pornography are limited to its erotic content, MacKinnon's critique is in terms of domination and the way images create a world of domination. This point must be clear for an accurate understanding of the following assessment of pornography:

> In pornography, there . . . is, in one place, all of the abuses that women had to struggle so long even to begin to articulate, all the *unspeakable* abuse: the rape, the battery, the sexual harassment, the prostitution, and the sexual abuse of children. Only in the pornography it is called something else: sex, sex, sex, sex, and sex, respectively. Pornography sexualizes rape, battery, sexual harassment, prostitution, and child sexual abuse; it thereby *celebrates, promotes, authorizes, and legitimizes them* [emphasis added]. More generally, it eroticizes the dominance and submission that is the dynamic common to them all. It makes hierarchy sexy and calls that "the truth about sex" or just a mirror reality. Through this process, pornography *constructs what a woman is as what men want from sex* [emphasis added]. This is what pornography means.[19]

To fully understand MacKinnon's position, a reader would do well to keep mentally adding the phrase "the images of" before each mention of pornography. These images are what celebrate, promote, authorize, and legitimize these dehumanizations of women and children. MacKinnon is sketching the human process by which a world of meaning is constructed that is counterhuman.

In the case of pornography, clusters of images become "a constitutive practice" of a theory of gender inequality:

> [P]ornography is neither harmless fantasy nor a corrupt and confused misrepresentation of an otherwise natural sexual situation. It institutionalizes sexuality of male supremacy, fusing the eroticization of dominance and submission with the social con-

struction of male and female. To the extent that gender is sexual, *pornography is part of constituting the meaning of that sexuality. Men treat women as who they see women as being* [emphasis added]. Pornography is that way.[20]

Applying these words to the question of imagery in general, we might say that what we see tends to construct a way of seeing and can even further become institutionalized in patterns of interaction between persons. Patterns of images can code our way of seeing. Would that those with explicit religious commitments understood the significance of this single point. Further, would that pastoral leaders could see its significance for themselves and the people in their congregations.

Images can — and indeed tend to — create assumptions about how the world really is. The verbs chosen by MacKinnon and found in my own comments get at the dynamism of images: institutionalizes, fusing, constituting, constructing, coding, creating. To put these verbs in the context of the title of this chapter: the material conditions of our seeing hold greater power in each of our lives than we ourselves tend to admit. As MacKinnon herself puts it, "Pornography ... is a political practice,"[21] to which I add, all depictions are a political practice, an exercise of power. Religious people do well to take notice and ask what it means for those who gather around an altar to proclaim God's gift in Jesus to find horrible, brutalizing images inoffensive, almost unnoticed.

Freedberg's, Miles's, and MacKinnon's claims about the particular power of images are disputed by many who control the production of images. Claims of the power of TV and film images are met with vigorous denials of their power. The daily press is filled with such denials.[22] I offer here one illustration of the image makers' contradictory claims. At the end of 1988, a controversy erupted in the media industry when the surgeon general's office planned a series of workshops on drunken driving that included data on the connection between drunken driving and advertising for alcohol.[23] Claiming there was no correlation between alcohol advertising and alcohol abuse, the American Association of Advertising Agencies objected to the conferences because of their fear the gatherings might lead to a ban on alcohol advertising. However, almost two and a half years later, the same advertising industry published statistical evidence of the effectiveness of their own public-service ads in persuading millions to become more aware of the causes of colon cancer and to be tested for the disease or to change habits that increased the risk of heart disease.[24] Eight months earlier, advertisers had taken out a full-page ad in widely circulated newspapers showing statistical evidence of ads' effectiveness in dissuading people from using drugs.[25]

The kinds of images MacKinnon holds up for scrutiny are not unknown to those in our local churches, and neither is the dominative behavior they foster, but her way of connecting the images to the attitudes of domination is rarely adverted to in church circles. Though denunciations of pornography may be common enough, the analysis of dehumanization in pornography is not so common. Perhaps church leaders have never had the chance to consider the power of images in the helpful ways Freedberg, Miles, or MacKinnon presents them. Once seen, this power needs the intelligent attention of religious people.[26]

Style as the Embracing of Impressions

So far I have been dealing with the images we see and how they can affect us. Here, in a move to a second set of studies of images, I wish to shift to the interplay between the images we see and the perceptions we have of our world and of ourselves in it. Some recent critiques of culture show how in our own century the conditions of our seeing have shifted our ways of naming reality. These shifts have religious implications.

The commentators I survey here all deal with a single feature of contemporary U.S. life: the preference of many people for appearances rather than substance, for impressions instead of thoughtfulness, for semblance over reality. Commentators use varied terminology to describe the same basic phenomenon. Stuart Ewen gives it the name "style." His use of the term differs from that of art historians, who mean by style the ornamental tastes elites succeed in having registered as the unified spirit of an age. Style today is a preoccupation of all sectors of society, but instead of the unified spirit of an age, it signifies almost the opposite. Style today draws its inspiration from any and all social sectors. As Ewen explains it in *All-Consuming Images: The Politics of Style in Contemporary Culture*,[27] style is all about surfaces, "mouthwatering" ones presented as material objects promising to free a life of the daily humdrum, allowing it to float beyond the terms of the real world. At almost every point the culture of surface, as described by Ewen, runs counter to the religious ethos: "Without ever saying so explicitly, the media of style offer to lift the viewer out of his or her life to be placed in a utopian netherworld where there are no conflicts, no needs unmet; where the ordinary is — by its very nature — extraordinary."[28] Like a fancy hat, style offers all a kind of surface prestige. Its virtuosity is exclusively skill in altering one's surface. Religious virtuosity, on the other hand, involves a transformation of the self toward God of such depth that it is assumed the transformation is indeed the work of God, more than of the one transformed. Its character is found in its stability, not its superficiality.

Using categories different from but basically in harmony with Mac-Kinnon's underlying critique of the way images construct a world, Ewen describes how these attitudes are communicated by ordinary televiewing, where the uninterrupted message is that style makes up a way of life, a utopian way marked by boundless wealth. The characters depicted most often dwell in a world of bounty, their living space sumptuously appointed, following their whims and fantasies effortlessly. Whatever the cost, paying for it is depicted as painless, with affordability not presented as an issue. Such illusions are essential to the enchantment of style, with its promise to swoop us out of the dreariness of necessity. At the other end of this tunnel of television, Ewen finds the viewer harassed by the actual conditions of life, where desire is in fact hemmed in by the constraints of circumstance. Exactly within such specific conditions is the viewer in a relationship with style. It is a quasi-religious relationship marked by promises of transcendence. Through the sorcery of style, the right consumer goods will transport one beyond the everyday to a dreamworld of perfection. If this analysis has any merit, it means that when some wander into the liturgical circle, these attitudes wander in with them. The analysis describes accurately the production of desire, an aspect of the production of consumption. Those who shape what we long for shape our spirits. Religious people who may intone the psalmist's words, "My heart longs for you, O Lord," do well to take note of this orchestration of desire in our time.

Style makes statements and even claims, but it has no convictions. Citing an ad for jeans, Ewen shows how the supposed "egalitarianism" of the product is underscored by information given about the blond, blue-eyed model: "Waitress, Bartender, Non-professional AIDS Educator, Cyclist, Art Restoration Student, Anglophile, Neo-Feminist." He comments: "In the world of style, ideas, activities, and commitments become ornaments, adding connotation and value to the garment while they are, simultaneously, eviscerated of meaning.... [Instead,] [m]odern style speaks to a world where change is the rule of the day, where one's place in the social order is a matter of perception, the product of diligently assembled illusions."[29] Ewen cautions us against seeing style as only a matter of subjectivity. Instead he wants us to understand how it is a social construct, created to support the centers of power in social, political, and economic life.

Most helpful in Ewen's account of style is his survey of the historical roots of contemporary attitudes toward it. That history goes back to the rise of the profit economy in medieval towns. As capital became a mobile form of wealth, merchants came to mimic the consumption practices of the nobility, which at first included elaborate clothing. The new merchant-class wealth looked to a variety of objects and products that might signal the status their wealth deserved. As style became something one could purchase, a new commerce in appearances emerged. Entrepreneurs devised ways of reproducing desirable books, such as lavishly illustrated Books of Hours, so as to make them more widely accessible to those who craved the status of owning them. When those with capital began to choose portraits as a way of signifying their status, art moved beyond the monasteries, churches, and castles. Various kinds of images and artwork became a form of social currency, something that advanced in the following centuries down to our own day. However, a key difference to emerge today is the ready access to the trappings of style, which Ewen calls the "iconography of prestige," due in large part to the capacity, perfected in the nineteenth century, for the cheap reproduction of this iconography.[30]

With signs of status cheaply available, a new kind of democracy developed, a consumer democracy, wherein most people had access to the styles once reserved for the elites. If not actual wealth, then "the coded look of wealth" came within the means of many. Machine-cut bric-a-brac glass could give the illusion of hand-cut fine glass. Factories developed processes of embossing and applying veneer that gave their products the look of quality. One commentator named these developments as the "delight in the unreal." Eventually even architecture adopted the separation of surface and substance in the way buildings were designed. The development of photography gave everyone except the very poorest accessibility to cheap images. According to Ewen, photography, of all the nineteenth-century developments, augmented the power of image over substance as a hallmark of modern style: "Photography became — almost immediately — a prime medium of pretension."[31] Photo studios could invest near paupers with the accoutrements of wealth and status they could then proudly display to others.

From this account one may understand why Ewen might emphasize the illusory or fake aspect of this culture of style:

> Style today is an incongruous cacophony of images, strewn across the social landscape. Style can be borrowed from any source and turn up in a place where it is least expected. The stylish person may look like a duchess one week, a murder victim the next. Style can hijack the visual idiom of astronauts or poach from the ancient pageantry of Guatemalan peasant costumes.[32]

Commenting in another place on style's illusory kind of change that in effect domesticates the human yearning for transformation, he writes,

> If the style market constitutes a presentation of a way of life, it is a way of life that is unattainable for most, nearly all, people. Yet this doesn't mean that style isn't relevant to most people. It is very relevant. It is the most common realm of our society in which the need for a better, or different, way of life is acknowledged, and expressed on a material level, if not met. It constitutes a politics of change, albeit a "change" that resides wholly on the surface of things. The surfaces, themselves, are lifted from an infinite number of sources.[33]

At issue here are quasi-religious promises about what is salvific in life and what can transport it to a new plane. At a polar opposite from religious transformation, the change has the depth of a glaze. The powerful way these promises are communicated can lead to their being unthinkingly accepted.

At this point some readers may be nervous about where my account of images today is leading. Is this an attack on the contemporary world? In every aspect of imagery is there a dangerous pothole ready to wrench religious wheels out of alignment? On the contrary, I wish to affirm every humanizing dimension of contemporary life. Actually I am a lover of images of all sorts, with special interest in film. My conviction is that religious persons have a right to examine contemporaneity from the stance of their religious commitments. Thoughtful religious people might ask questions like these: When people assemble for worship, do the attitudes Ewen describes assemble with them? Do these attitudes provide the unnamed hermeneutical context of worship, possibly overriding the stipulated context or at least quietly undermining it? Do any of the quasi-religious promises about what is salvific worm their way into the homily? Can catechesis as a ministry to communal practice provide critical tools to assist people to assess these false promises? Under what conditions may religious worship itself, intent on distancing the truth of God from idolatrous falsehoods, be a zone where people may creatively confront cultural illusions? Is the proper Christian response to the superficiality of the culture of surface a kind of "productive noncontemporaneity?"[34]

Behind everything Ewen writes is the idea that people today have a penchant to copy in their own persons the images presented to them. They are being invited to adopt any surface; what they appear to be is who they are. The astonishing proliferation of surgery to alter appearance, that is, cosmetic surgery, is one example of this adoption of surface now come to roost in every neighborhood, with a fair amount of it being done for teens. Of the 643,910 cosmetic surgery procedures performed in the United States in 1990, "breast augmentations" ranked second at 89,402, right behind "fat de-augmentation," or liposuction, at 109,080.[35] Ralph Lauren's claim that he does not sell clothes but dreams is another example of the marketing of surfaces.[36]

One could ask, But isn't this good, to question what reality is? Doesn't our Enlightenment penchant to divide the world into the real and unreal allow us to distinguish areas of life as fantasy or as unscientific but still useful? Yes, such matters are complex. One could argue that the young woman who adopts one surface one week and another surface the week after is actually saying, "The real me is the person underneath, and you can't get at that person only via appearances." Yes, in this sense her consciousness has a positive side. The negative side appears when and if she thinks, "You can't know the real me unless I give this particular appearance." Or, "If I have one life to live, I must live it with this particular kind of surgically adjusted nose." Can grief over one's body be manipulated by commercial interests, and if so, how humanly diminishing is that grief?[37] Authenticity in life has to do with the coherence between who I seem to be and who I actually am and also with my self-defining commitments. Religiously, authenticity has to do with who I am when I stand before God, a stance that allows imagination to be, as Auden put it, "redeemed from promiscuous fornication with her own images." Authenticity does not come from those forces manipulating the self in the interests of profit.

Ewen is pointing out the centrality of mimesis, of imitative behavior, in our day. I had always known that children were busy copying behavior as their major lifework at the earliest ages. It took me some while to realize that young people between the ages of twelve and twenty-two are also very busy copying or searching, sometimes frantically, for models to copy. Finally I came to see the drive for imitation as a central but underexamined and underestimated character of all human life.[38] In the early 1990s one journalist explored the way the TV series *L.A. Law* had influenced the U.S. legal profession,[39] while another explained the way the old *Perry Mason* TV show had influenced current courtroom procedures in Italy. In religious traditions, such as the Jewish and Christian ones, imitation of virtuoso religious attainments is given a special — but explicit — value. But Ewen's description of imitative "style" discloses imitation reduced to its least possibilities. The creation of illusory "realities" has another dimension religious people need to consider.

If an organizing principle of our former industrial society was production, in today's postindustrial society it is simulation. Industrial production was able to crank out in series products that were exact replicas of one another, first through human-labor assembly lines and later through automation. Through this process the original kind of simulation, the one-of-a-kind copy or counterfeit, has long been supplanted by multiple copies. These replicas were in a sense simulations but in a qualitatively different degree from today's simulations. Just as machine-produced replicas were a quantum leap from the original copy, so today's simulations are a similar leap from machine copies. In fact, in the current world of simulations, all reference to the real has been replaced. Now models create a "real" that has no true reference to reality or to origins.[40]

For example, Ralph Lauren has created in his New York City headquarters a two-story atrium paneled in mahogany, designated not the reception area but The Reading Room, which one commentator called "a more perfectly wrought version of a 19th century London men's club, or of the library of a great country house, than exists anywhere in the real world."[41] The writer goes on to ask, "What is more real — the imaginary men's club of the Reading Room, or the real ones it is modeled after?" Of his rustic fantasy PoloLauren Country Store in East Hampton, New York, we are told "no better stage-set version of an old country store [exists] anywhere:"

> You are walking through a miniature theme park of Americana, filled with attractive pieces of clothing, any one of which you can have if you only present a credit card. You're not buying a shirt, you're buying into a life style. With Ralph Lauren, you don't need blue-blooded forebears any more than you need a wardrobe adviser or an interior decorator. Mr. Lauren provides you with the whole package, guaranteed to pass muster.[42]

The simulated character of much contemporary life poses a special challenge able to be met by religious groups, whose sacred texts and traditions face their adherents with forceful questions about the nature of reality and the nature of falseness. However, they must first come to see the problem and its religious implications.

Someone might at this point object that I have made my point about the culture of surface and the problem of simulation in our day. In my mind's ear, I hear the shout, "Enough, already!" My own sense, however, is that the issues here so deeply affect a religious sense and are so capable of undermining it, they must be pondered at length. As I have already stressed, this book is not a denunciation of contemporary culture, far from it, but it points out how needed in such a culture are communities whose religious practice can offer a countervailing sensibility in a time of illusion.

I have already, in another place, laid out some of the skills needed for what I called "cultural analysis:" the ability of religious people to analyze the production of meaning and of meaning-laden images and, where necessary, their effects on human sensibility.[43] The basic point is that religious symbols and meanings are to be consciously embraced as key tools for decoding the world and actively used in our encounter with the world. Too often, this particular connection between religious images and the wider world of images is not made. I know a devout Buddhist family who meditate every morning at a living-room shrine to the Buddha sitting in his quiet pose of contemplation. Yet, if the children's claim to have seen all the Schwarzenegger films is true, it shows that not all religious persons adequately consider the contradictions that may exist between their religious faith and the films they see.

The Culture of Surface: Further Corroboration

In a kind of summary of his study, Ewen contrasts the medieval production of images with their production today:

> Modern style speaks to a world where change is the rule of the day, where one's place in the social order is a matter of perception, the product of diligently assembled illusions.... Style speaks for a society in which coherent meaning has fled to the hills, and in which drift has provided a context of continual discontent....
> The production of sumptuous images, for the very few, was once limited to the sacred workshops of the medieval monasteries; now,

the production and marketing of style is global, touching the lives
and imaginations of nearly everyone.[44]

These convictions are borne out by two journalists working independently of one another in the United States. Reporting on a Manhattan
dinner party, Barbara Goldsmith identifies the celebrity guests as including a U.S. senator, an embezzler, a woman said to spend $60,000
a year on flowers, the host of a talk show, the chief executive officer
of one of the nation's largest corporations, a writer who had settled a
plagiarism suit, and a Nobel laureate. Goldsmith points out that such
an assemblage blurs the distinction between fame and notoriety, between talent and its lack, between accomplishment and merely being
well-known, between heroes and villains.[45] What these persons had in
common was celebrity status. They all gave an "image" or impression
of some quality: wealth, success, heroism, glamour, leadership, danger. When such synthetic personalities become heroes, it is a sign a
society is absenting itself from the ethical judgment needed for social health. Goldsmith warns, "We no longer demand reality, only that
which is real-seeming."[46] Since the characteristics of a society are found
in those it celebrates, an increasing lack of concern about the qualifications of these celebrities has ominous portent. Beyond the preference
it shows for synthetic persons vicariously acting out a society's noblest
and basest desires, it portends a preference for illusion over reality.
Goldsmith warns,

> In today's highly technological world, reality has become a pallid
> substitute for the image reality we fabricate for ourselves, which
> in turn intensifies our addiction to the artificial. Anyone who has
> attended a political convention or a major sporting event knows
> that watching the proceedings on television, where cameras highlight the most riveting moments, then replay and relate them in
> similar situations, provides us with more stimulating and complex perceptions than being there does. Next year's visitors to the
> Grand Canyon need not see it. One mile from the boundary will
> be a $5 million complex where they will be able to view a film
> of the way the Canyon looks during all four seasons and take a
> simulated raft ride through artificial rapids.[47]

And so the mechanically recorded and technically altered reality has
greater value than the actuality.

Kennedy Fraser, a journalist specializing in fashion, picks up the same theme from her own perspective — but only after stepping out of her usual role of commenting about the fashion industry and turning to critique fashion itself. Fraser finds that in its deepest sense fashion is about something more significant than couture or frivolities of taste. Neither named or noted, it is rather "the lens through which our society perceives itself and the mold to which it increasingly shapes itself."[48] Hidden and unacknowledged, this mental kind of fashion needs to be brought into the light and evaluated. Mental fashion has much in common with the frivolous, pirouetting, old kind of fashion — that of dress: both hold appearances to be of greater significance than substance. "Among [their] shared limitations are fickleness, a preoccupation with descrying the will of the majority in order to manipulate it or pander to it, and a concern with the accumulation or protection of power and profit." Though often passing itself off as rebellious, fashion actually works to support power: "to think or act for reasons of fashion in any given field is to support that field's established centers of power."

Fraser is describing the nose for trend in the search for "the right stuff," not in the sense of the correct clothing styles but rather of the right ideas, the right interests, the right values, even the right spiritual concerns. Mental fashion is a "skilled master of enthusiasm" causing many to overlook how slavishly they in fact follow along. Even those who should be fostering quality, individuality, and the ability to reflect — writers, critics, artists, editors, and so forth — are apt to present ideas and facts as trendy commodities. They thus help society hand itself over to trend and style as worthy guides of the human project. Fraser warns that when fashion becomes the framework for perception, it warps not only perception but any reasonable picture of the world:

> The greatest drawback of an overfashionable perception is that fashion is concerned, virtually by definition, with surfaces, images, appearances.... When the mind surrenders itself to fashion, the first casualty is objective judgment — which is, to all intents, the mind itself. Fashionable perception is incapable of discerning any fixed truth about an object or event.[49]

Intelligence, on the other hand, demands honest, disinterested distinctions, "born of an isolated, dogged, unfashionable side of the mind — a sort of gawky mental provincialism." If the word "appreciative" were added to that list of adjectives, they would describe not just intelligence but religious intelligence. Ironically, the market for mental fashion is especially vital among the college educated who, having tasted intellectual activity, are now nostalgic for the literary enthusiasms of studenthood. As a result, society comes to pattern itself on fashion.

My initial reading of Goldsmith's and Fraser's ideas set me on a course of study over a period of more than ten years and got me pondering how people's perceptions are shaped and what influence on perception religious assemblies actually have. Of course, Goldsmith and Fraser reinforce Ewen's main positions. These thinkers and others like them represent a form of cultural critique that describes a current situation in enough detail to engage the concern of religious people of any major tradition. They support and flesh out the positions of David Freedberg, Margaret Miles, and Catharine MacKinnon. Still the questions remain. What can be done about this marketing of and embracing of illusion, of surfaces, about this preferring impression over reflection, or about the promise of salvation from the right commodities? What does this situation mean for religious people — and their leaders — living in the same society and culture described by our commentators? In the face of the socially fostered preference for illusion, will religious people be able to hold to their unique understandings and judgments about reality — to their "gawky religiously humanizing provincialism"? If recognition of a problem is a major step toward dealing with it, these commentators on the culture of illusion, all secular writers, offer religious people much assistance. By the way they live, that is, by their communal practice of their sacred texts, local churches can provide, though not easily, an alternative zone from which to reflect on the purpose of life as imagined by Jesus. In addition, preaching and catechesis may find ways to give people the tools to decode and, where appropriate, contest images and image systems.

The ability to embrace the implications of our verbal claims is one of these tools. When what we say in our ritual prayer does not engage our imagination and deeper convictions, those ritual words are inert. But when these words have implications vital to us in our approach to the world, they have their proper active, even turbulent, character. As a child, I was impressed by the many times my mother pointed out to us the discrepancy between what we had just said and done in church and our behavior toward one another once we got home. Pointing to the sign of unity and love implicit in receiving the Eucharist, she expected us to live that sign in the way we interacted with one another. She saw that the ritual's truth about us was not meant to be inert but to engage us, with implications for behavior. On reflection, I now see she was pointing to a central religious dilemma regarding truth claims: Will they be active and engaging or inert? She had resolved this dilemma for herself on the side of active engagement.

All human practice is rooted in the primal practices of gesture and language. When our practice of religious language ignores the material conditions of our seeing, that language practice colludes in enabling the conditions of our seeing to go unnoticed. That practice implies the matter is unimportant. On the other hand, attention to the conditions of our seeing, along with the empowerment that can emerge from it, will be broadly based, not so much in "courses" as in communal dialogue about the way of looking at reality called for by our own sacred texts and about the cultural power latent in that most sacramental of texts, the life of the local church. Pulpit ranting about the evils of secular culture has zero effect, and rightly so. The issue is not denunciation but a renewed embracing of our own Jesus-inspired, inconvenient way of responding to God at this time and in this place. The lively embodiment of this Christic imagination is sacramental for the life of the assembly and all who come into contact with it.

Frederic Jameson asks the very question many readers at this point may be raising for themselves: How will it be possible for those immersed in these image systems to separate out for themselves a moment of truth from the many moments of illusion? He suggests the possibility that the material conditions of our seeing, even when we become aware of them, may tend "to demobilize us and to surrender us to passivity and helplessness" because of their seeming historical inevitability.[50] Indeed Jameson himself suggests that culture is no longer an area of social life that can be considered separate from economics or politics. In our time he finds "a prodigious expansion of culture throughout the social realm, to the point at which everything in our social life — from economic value and state power to practices and to the very structure of the psyche itself — can be said to have become 'cultural' in some original and as yet untheorized sense."[51] All cultural "space" has been taken over and colonized by the logic of late capitalism.

Jameson believes the new situation can be countered only by means of a new kind of activity he calls "a radical cultural politics." His proposed new form of human agency is grounded in cognitive mapping, an activity analogous to the mapping of urban space. An alienated city is a space where people are unable to map in their own minds either their positions in the city or their relationship to the city as a whole. Such a city is lacking markers, like monuments or boundaries, like parks or road patterns, that allow people to see where they are. Urban mapping disalienates because it discloses the human construction of urban space hidden to the casual observer. Similarly, cognitive mapping disalienates because it shows persons their relationships to their wider social space: their cultural space.[52]

I find merit in Jameson's suggestion for cognitive mapping — vague as it is. He admits it is an idea that needs to be worked out in concrete strategies. The idea, however, involves helping people understand how images work, how they are produced and communicated, and who profits from them. The idea also involves making judgments about what we see from informed points of view, such as a religiously informed point of view. Images tend to be ineffable, beyond words, but they need not be. They can be investigated, decoded, analyzed, commented on, interpreted, judged, and contested as untrue or false or dishonest.

In reading Jameson, I found myself thinking of another kind of space, the space inhabited by those gathered around an altar as a sacred space uniting them to all others as children of God. This space, and the imagery brought to bear there on all of life, offers those gathered a fundamental point of orientation in their perception of reality and in their relation to the world. Because of its claims to ultimacy, here is a "cognitive map" of potentially transformative power. Above, I gave an example of a mother's insistence on the factual ultimacy of those claims. But will religious persons embrace this power to free themselves from false imaginations of what human existence is meant to be? Indeed, this power is at some level a natural part of the human condition, as W. H. Auden reminds us in his prescient Christmas oratorio, *For the Time Being*, published in 1945. We cannot totally hide from what is actual; somewhere, sometime, it will press in on us:

> If we were never alone or always too busy,
> Perhaps we might even believe what we know is not true:
> But no one is taken in, at least not all of the time;
> In our bath, or the subway, or the middle of the night,
> We know very well we are not unlucky but evil,
> That the dream of a Perfect State or No State at all,
> To which we fly for refuge, is a part of our punishment.[53]

Questions for Discussion and Reflection

1. The author claims pastoral workers are well aware of the images of their own religious tradition but marginally aware of the images people see in their everyday lives. What is your position on this matter, and what evidence would you bring forward to justify it?

2. Freedberg says people today discount the power of images, hiding from themselves the actual power of visual images. Do you find any examples of this claim in the way images affect children? How do images affect people your own age?

3. Catharine MacKinnon's writing on dominative exploitation in pornography has sparked great controversy, particularly from women. Do any of her claims ring true to you? Which ones?

4. Stuart Ewen's commentary on all-consuming images is laced with subtle references to the salvific promises of images. How useful do you find his analysis for understanding what is influencing our people?

5. What implications does Ewen's critique have for the kind of spirituality (meaning, the total direction of their human spirit) people today are living and for pastoral work in spirituality?

6. The last section of the chapter deals with the problem today of what is real and the challenge of fostering a countervailing religious sensibility in a time of illusion. Does this challenge overstate the power of religious communities? Are there conditions under which such communities affect the way we look at the world? Can we name such religious assemblies?

7. This chapter addressed the relation between the way people imagine their lives and the way they live their lives — and the implications for religious people. Did the chapter help you think about the problem, clarify it, confuse you, frustrate you? Is there any action you need to take after reading it?

Examining Images

1. Are there common metaphors or comparisons that some in your local church readily accept that others cannot accept? For example, what might be examples of metaphoric images that women will not accept but men will, or that men will not accept but

women will? Are there metaphors used in your community that seem to you ill-advised? Are there kinds of filmed or televised images that children will accept but adults will not — or vice versa? Are there images the well-off find comforting but the poor find painful? What are these?

2. When was the last time your community publicly considered the question of images?

3. What are some films you consider ill-suited for children? To teens and young adults; to adults; to anyone? What are films you find to have special merit for each of these age groups?

4. How can a congregation raise for itself the question of criteria for film and television? Are there any ways to surface questions about film and TV that might be helpful to community members?

5. How do people of various ages in your congregation go about deciding what films they will see in a movie theater? How do they decide what videos they will rent or purchase?

6. Are there images you use in worship whose significance is generally overlooked? What would be some examples? How can these images become more significant to your congregation?

CHAPTER THREE

THE LOCAL CHURCH AND ITS PRACTICE OF THE GOSPEL

The Materiality of Discipleship in a Catechesis of Liberation

I TELL UNDERGRADUATE STUDENTS in a course on Christian marriage that if I wanted to know who they really are, I would need very specific kinds of information. If they would supply me with the following documents and facts, I could "read their tea leaves" and tell them what they are all about:

- their checkbook

- a list of books, magazines, and other printed material they read over the past week or month

- indication of whether or not they watch TV and, if so, a list of what and how they watch

- a list, naming the place and event, of the tickets they buy

- their phone bills

- a record of the kinds of liquids they consume and under what circumstances they do so

- their credit-card bills

- a list of their ways of spending leisure time

- a description of their patterns of eating

- the mileage of their commute to work or school

- a description of their pattern, or lack of pattern, of religious practice

My students are quick to point out that if they had the same information about me, they would also be able to "read" me. But does such
reading extend to the church? How do we go about reading the church
or a congregation? Do we examine the writings and teachings of the
church? How does it use its resources, including its money? What role
does practice play?

What happens around the altar or in the space of worship has
potential for a radical reimagination of the world, realizable when a
community is willing to face the implications of its words and deeds
of worship. However the space of worship can also be a space of con-
tradiction. In an essay on Christian initiation in the Episcopal Church,
William Adams explores the place of baptism by examining the use of
space and the use of ritual in a sampling of Episcopal parishes.[1] Adams
probes whether the symbolic ritual enactments, both in their use of
space and in the ritual unfolding itself, back up the church's stated convictions about the key place of baptism. Officially, the baptismal pool or
font, in keeping with its importance in the community's total life, is to
have a significant place in the space where the community assembles.
Thus there are to be three key areas in the space where the community assembles for worship: the altar, the pulpit from which the Word
is announced, and the place of baptism. Adams's study sought to determine whether the place of baptism was in fact spatially significant. The
study also scrutinized the ritual of baptism as practiced, contrasting the
ritual of ordination with that of baptism to see the assumptions embedded in each and whether the practice of these rituals squares with
stated teaching that baptism is to have greater significance. In the way
the rituals are actually carried out, he found that the "physical observable evidence" shows ordination has much greater significance, at least
when examined as ritual action. Studying *actual practice* rather than
stated theoretical positions, Adams finds what the church does in this
ritual to be not fully coherent with its teachings.[2]

This chapter seeks to lay out in more detail the significance of the
material conditions of church practice, a significance that is difficult to
overstate, for as Marianne Sawicki suggests, these conditions determine
our capacity for recognizing the Risen Lord.[3] Adams's study examines
whether what we practice is what we proclaim in our official teachings, and focuses on *the teaching represented by the practice*. The rest of
this book presses on this point. The teaching embedded in patterns of
behavior lived but not reflected on will be an issue for all in pastoral
ministry, particularly Christian educators or catechists, especially if we

accept that what a community lives is at least as formative as what it teaches about itself.

Here I will build on the dilemmas sketched in chapter 1 of how to translate religious vision into a life practice true to that vision and in chapter 2 of how our religious commitment can help us interpret the images we see. I wish to lay a groundwork for considering what might be called "the symbolics of practice" at the level, not of liturgical symbolics, but of life-structure symbolics. What people say and do in the liturgical assembly, including the arrangement of space in which they say and do it, provides clues to what these people are all about. However — and this is a central point in my argument — what they say and do in the nonliturgical spaces of their individual and corporate lives has a more decisive effect on them than does liturgical speech and action, for there we find the physical, observable evidence of actual commitments. The material structures of their lives have already formed them — their consciousness, their mentality, their biases, their priorities, their spirit — before they cross the threshold of liturgical space.

At this juncture, I wish to clarify a key point about the relationship between what we say and what we do. The character of the human is found in a vision of one's life that exceeds possible actualization. Karl Rahner's theology is founded on the human as open to the more. This character can be found in the press for ever-improved standards in athletics, in the call of leaders like Martin Luther King Jr. to his people to engage the struggle for human betterment, and even in those who adopt various personae via the magic of fashion. It is certainly at the heart of the marketing industry's manipulation of human desire. Even in a colleague's complaint, "I'm just not myself today," we find this struggle towards who we are meant to be. In this book, I am seeking neither the "perfect church" nor fully realized, "finished" discipleship. As far as I am concerned, there is no such thing. Discipleship is not a static reality; it exists only in its never-ending struggle for fidelity. The problem I am trying to raise is what happens when we forget or do not recognize the distance between what we say and what we do or between what we are now and what we know we are summoned to be. When the life of the local church encourages this forgetting, often by means of self-congratulation, something at the heart of Jesus' proposals has been lost. Thinking nice thoughts is not the goal of Christian life.

Though attention to this matter is growing, I find it insufficient, especially in the literature of catechetics, which should be focused more on practices than on concepts. Even those who purport to deal with shaping the practice of particular ecclesial groups do not deal with either liturgical symbolics in Adams's sense or life-practice symbolics in my sense. Storytelling as a technique of formation or of re-formation of the assembly is not sufficient for coping with the kind of life practice I seek to address here.[4] As I noted in chapter 1, one of the few Christian education theorists who has gotten at the issue of the life practice of local churches is C. Ellis Nelson in his *Where Faith Begins*.[5] Marianne Sawicki's *Seeing the Lord: Resurrection and Early Christian Practices* is the most stimulating recent treatment of ecclesial practice I know of.[6] Edward Farley's writings consistently raise the issue for scholars and students of theology.

Practice surfaces in Roman Catholic catechetical documents and, I presume, in those of all the denominations, but the matter has still not been brought forward in a cohesive way that highlights its key place in Christian education/catechesis. Here, to get at the importance of practice and some reasons why it is neglected, I begin with one of the few places where practice is raised consistently and forcefully: the literature of liberation theology.[7] I will suggest some further work necessary if the material conditions of practice are to receive the emphasis they deserve in the church and in pastoral ministry.

Our Way and Our Say

In the very first paragraph of his now-classic work *A Theology of Liberation*, Gustavo Gutiérrez explains how every ecclesial community has built into its way of life a rough outline of a theological understanding. The "life, action, and concrete attitude" found in the community provide the soil into which theological reflection "sinks its roots and from which it derives its strength."[8] Though never stressing the negative side of this principle — that this soil could be the source of a community's shallow ineptitude — Gutiérrez implies that the material conditions of the community's life can be for good or ill. The title of the book's first chapter, "Theology: A Critical Reflection," means not so much Gutiérrez's critical reflection on theology but rather that theology itself is done as a critical reflection on the concrete circumstances of the local church's life. Rarely do local congregations achieve this goal. "[T]he *very life of the Church* [emphasis his] . . . [is] a *locus theologicus*, "that is, a zone for doing theological reflection.[9] Throughout this opening chapter he stresses the importance "of concrete behavior, of deeds, of action, of praxis in the Christian life."[10]

The goal of reflection on the material conditions of life is to fashion a practice of the gospel worked out in a probing examination of a community's economic and sociocultural circumstances. Far from downplaying doctrine and tradition, liberation theology employs them in fashioning a concrete practice of discipleship that rescues truth and wisdom from becoming static and sterile. This specific practice is sacramental in a positive or a negative way; it either brings to life the community's faith in God, or it helps numb that faith. Where practice is life-giving, the community relentlessly asks, Does our way square with our say?

Understood thus, liberation theology seeks the local church as both an accessible sign of the presence of God's promised Christ and a habitable sign. Neither feature is easily attained. An accessible sign is different from a simply "claimed" or purported sign because one can see what the accessible sign stands for; the way the sign functions makes its meaning tangible and sense-able. A habitable sign invites one to live its meanings in communion, as others do. In the early 1960s when I tried for several years to teach ecclesiology to skeptical teens, I found their unavoidable stumbling block to be, not the claims of the church, but the lack of coherence between those claims and actual concrete life practice of the local parish.[11] The way did not square with the say. The young found the embodiments of my ecclesial theory to be neither accessible nor habitable. In so finding, they verified Joseph Komonchak's description of ecclesiology as "a theory about a practice";[12] the ecclesiology I was presenting was a theory about a theory, not about a practice. I came to see that the most convincing way of presenting the theory of the church was to ground it in a convincing practice — which at that time was an alternative practice.[13]

Fewer than four years after Gutiérrez's book appeared in its first Spanish edition, an important papal statement backed up his basic position. In December 1975, *Evangelii Nuntiandi* appeared over the signature of Paul VI, as a papal response to the issues raised at the 1974 Synod of Bishops on the issue of evangelization. Though Roman Catholic in origin, this document has universal significance for all Christians. Opening with several anguished questions about the possibilities of proclaiming the gospel in our day, the exhortation returns again and again to the matter of the church as an accessible and credible sign. The very first step of evangelization is for the church itself to be evangelized and converted to God, becoming a community of believers making real their hope through loving-kindness to others.[14] Evangelized itself, the church finds its foundational way of evangelizing others to be by means of witness: the sign of an ecclesia embracing the humanizing vision of the gospel and living not only in communion with its own members but in solidarity with all seeking what is "noble and good." Such witness is basically "wordless" but deeply provocative, that is, raising questions about the vision and intent of those living this way, and renders God's presence accessible to others in tangible signs.[15] Near its conclusion, the document uses vivid language of self-confrontation:

> Either tacitly or aloud — but always forcefully — we are being asked: Do you really believe what you are proclaiming? Do you live what you believe? Do you really preach what you live? The witness of life has become more than ever an essential condition for real effectiveness in preaching.[16]

Here *Evangelii Nuntiandi* echoes Thomas Finn's statement cited in the first chapter: "[T]he cardinal principle that permeated early catechetics was that any belief not embodied in conduct was not true belief."[17]

Implied, however, in *Evangelii Nuntiandi's* description of a believable ecclesial community is a process of struggle whereby a group seeks to embrace specific patterns of practice by which a gospel perspective can be lived out in its concrete circumstances. The conversion of the community sparked by its encounter with the message of Jesus is not a onetime ecstatic event based on euphoric insight into "truth." Translating conversion into patterns of practice that go beyond ritual enactments of the tradition and become embedded in specific ways of living is no euphoric matter. In fact it is the opposite. Ecstasy means standing outside the self, being lifted out of the self. Establishing gospel living in a specific set of circumstances involves standing, not outside the self or the community, but squarely within one's materiality, one's embodiedness within networks of particularities. Ultimately, as we shall see, gospel practice involves judgments and decisions about a range of life practices.

Resistance to the Issue of Life Structure

Middle- and upper-class ecclesial communities have for the most part not faced the challenge of specific life practice. One way to support this claim is simply to note the lack of pastoral literature on the matter. In all fields of human endeavor can be found studied interest in standards of practice, with practitioners ready to submit themselves to the best standard so far achieved. This interest in practice and readiness to examine and learn from virtuoso performance can be found in sports, in the arts, in the crafts, even in management theory. Among those who work to hone a particular kind of human skill, any field of practice demands this kind of relatedness among practitioners, involving mutual examination and evaluation — and consequent appreciation or criticism. Basically, "we cannot be initiated into a practice without accepting the authority of the best standards realized so far."[18] This is as true for the playing of the French horn as it is for the practice of virtue.

Quite simply, in pastoral theology the literature showing this interest in practice hardly exists. There is ample literature, called "pastoral theology" or "practical theology," about the theory of practice but with little to say about the wider patterns of action that make up a specific structure of life for any person or community. There is also a literature of case studies, valuable in themselves, but these tend to focus on a minister's pastoral skills while offering little critical reflection on or even attention to the concrete social conditions of living within which the pastoral skills function.[19] When the problematic of practice surfaces in these studies, it is not the problem of the specific kinds of life patterns embedded in the local community, say, patterns of rampant consumerism — what one could term "operational greed" — being lived out by the majority in the community.

Though patterns of behavior can pass into repetitive, embedded practice without ever going through discourse, they cannot, as Pierre Bourdieu warns us, be contested and changed apart from the intentionality that goes with discourse.[20] In many churches persons have been empowered to speak knowledgeably about their sacred texts and about those texts' meaning for their interior life. Many, however, do not have a language by which to apply the texts to the patterns of exteriority in their lives, to the way they spend time, money, attention, and energies, or to the stream of visual images they see daily. These patterns, both among individuals and in the church's own corporate life, are outside of discourse. When practices, for example, those of consumerist greed, are ignored, they tend to generate their own false theory of Christian living, a theory that supposes gospel fidelity to be unconnected to the use of money. Remember Jacques Ellul's caution that false practice can generate false theory but in a particularly subtle and stubborn way (see p. 14). [21] We continue to maintain our stated "theory," when in fact it has been replaced by an unacknowledged operational theory derived from false practice. With the ease of the child in "The Emperor's New Clothes," my secondary school students of yesteryear objected that the actual ecclesiology in force in their churches was quite different from the stated "theoretical" ecclesiology. Practice of any kind may encode in our lives values and attitudes we may never wish consciously to admit to ourselves. We are unwilling to see or decode what we ourselves have written into our own lives.

If it is true that one is what one does, then patterns of action determine the sort of person one becomes. The issue of whether and how action does create personhood has been continually thrust in our faces during the last half of the twentieth century. The ongoing prosecution of crimes against humanity, particularly committed by the Nazis and by non-Nazi soldiers in Hitler's army, has pressed many to examine the connection between one's actions and one's human spirit. Many indicted for war crimes have defended themselves as having just behaved as good soldiers, acting under orders from above. And "those above" have in turn defended themselves as also having acted on order from *above them*. Rarely have those found guilty asked for forgiveness. The continual examination of these questions forces us all to recognize the significance of action. It is a matter that will not go away. Even in nations where the brutality of the military was legally sanctioned during atrocities and then legally absolved afterwards, the memory of injustice is kept alive as are the names of those who never accepted responsibility for their deeds.[22]

Not all our patterns of action are consciously chosen; many are simply fallen into, adopted through unspoken social permission or initiated in choices made but not examined, choices that bypass discourse. Often initiated without thought or even innocently, these patterns are not maintained without our own complicity. Whatever their origin in choice, all patterns shape the human spirit and a way of being an embodied spirit, that is, a spirituality.[23] At some point in its activity, religiousness must reflect on not just its system of meanings but on the conditions under which these meanings can be realized in concrete behavior. The word "conditions" here is important because it suggests that behavior is not simply individual but also contextual and social. One could ask, Under what conditions do persons claiming discipleship with Jesus come to overlook the consequences of their deeds for that discipleship — if not all deeds, then at least whole categories of deeds? These conditions for overlooking or attending to deeds are my concern here.

Why has the liberationist concern with concrete patterns of behavior not been taken up by the churches of privilege? Historical or tradition-laden reasons present themselves, as well as more immediate ones. Paulo Freire suggests to me one of the more immediate ones. In a brief comment, he notes one of the conclusions of a UNESCO-sponsored international meeting on adult literacy: that programs of adult literacy "have been efficient in societies in which suffering and change created a special motivation in the people for reading and writing."[24] In other words, social conditions of suffering create among some a need for literacy not felt by those illiterates who are more comfortable. In a similar way, the positions of privilege occupied by those in the churches of the well-off and very well-off do not spark the need for change. Among those of privilege, the conditions of prosperity hinder their probing the religious implications of these same conditions of prosperity.

To be sure, all patterns of practice tend to be taken for granted and invisible until the pattern is somehow disrupted. Patterns of spending money become sharply visible when the money dries up; patterns of using transportation, when one's means of transportation breaks down; patterns of eating, when medical imperatives demand change. However, to repeat a claim made throughout this book, built into the very nature of religious meaning is the possibility of calling into question patterns of practice. Religious meanings claim to be ultimate ones, worth suffering for, normative for living. Though this aspect of religiousness is not always called into play or can be muted, the claim of ultimacy remains embedded in religious traditions, and its latent implications for living are always capable of being activated.

Religions are not simply ways of thinking; they are also and especially ways of living. Their religious understandings are to become lived realities. Practice remains the test of adherence to the religious system. In another of his writings, Gutiérrez explains the prominence of practice for Christianity:

> Practice is the locus of verification of our faith in God, who liberates by establishing justice and right in favor of the poor. It is also the locus of verification of our faith in Christ.... Easter life is the life of practice.... The only faith-life is the one the Scriptures call "Witness." And witness is borne in works. To believe is to practice.
>
> Only from a point of departure at the level of practice, only from deed, can the proclamation by word be understood. In the deed our faith becomes truth, not only for others, but for our-

selves as well. We become Christians by acting as Christians. Proclamation in word only means taking account of this fact and proclaiming it. Without the deed, proclamation of the word is something empty, something without substance.

... [T]he relationship between deed and word is asymmetric. What basically counts is the deed. Of course it will not do to overemphasize this or push it to extremes; its only purpose is the better to express a complex reality. Jesus Christ, the heart of the gospel message, is the Word made flesh, the Word become deed. Only in this unity of deed and word is there any sense in the distinctions we make in the task of proclaiming liberation in Jesus Christ.[25]

This relationship of word and deed, of understanding and practice, has not always been maintained in Christianity, and residues of earlier misunderstandings remain in the tradition. How these misunderstandings emerged must now be examined.

Pieris's Analysis of the Displacement of Agape

The Jesuit theologian Aloysius Pieris reminds us that any religion must combine both loving action (agape) and the search for wisdom (gnosis). Along the roadsides of his own country, Sri Lanka, he finds two sets of statues that spell out for him the importance of the unification of loving action and quiet wisdom. Each statue involves a tree, one symbolizing knowledge, the other, love-in-action:

the tree beneath which Gotama, the Indian mystic, sits in a posture of contemplative calm, and the tree upon which Jesus the Hebrew prophet hangs in a gesture of painful protest — ... the tree that bears the fruit of wisdom and the tree that bares the cost of love.[26]

For encountering God and for expressing the fruits of our intimacy with God, each, agape and gnosis, is important. Together they represent "complementary idioms that need each other to mediate the self-transcending experience called salvation..."; any valid spirituality, Buddhist or Christian ... retains both poles of religious experience, the gnostic and the agapeic."[27] Pieris's analysis of the functioning of the agapeic and the gnostic poles brings to light a historical irony, that the religion using the gnostic symbol of the tree of wisdom, Buddhism, has been able to hold on to the actual practice of love and the one using the agapeic symbol, Christianity, has tended to emphasize a particular gnostic strain. Pieris explains how this occurred.

In its early formative centuries, Christianity found itself in a gnostic milieu tending to assert that knowing the liberating truth is salvation. From the first, Christianity was able to find a theological formula able to maintain the gnostic pole without compromising the agapeic. The theologies of John and Paul, according to Pieris, give concrete evidence of this formula. In John, the knowledge of the Father and the Son is given by the Spirit but leads to a discipleship that is a concrete way of loving one's neighbor. Here loving one's neighbor is the way of knowing God. One finds a similar bonding of knowledge and love in Paul's emphasis on otherly love:

> Paul admits the possibility of knowing divine things but clearly considers such knowledge worthless without love. Paul puts a greater distance than John between *ginoskein* and *agapan* as between two different modes of human experience. But one can infer that for both [i.e., John and Paul] the Sinai covenant of justice has received its final fulfillment in Jesus in whom mutual love among humans is the path to true gnosis — the knowledge of God through the Son in the Spirit.[28]

The wedding of these two elements was maintained in the carefully monitored catechumenal process of the early church, with its emphasis on helping neophytes restructure their patterns of living. As we have seen, the catechumenate was a method of formation, not just in doctrinal purity, but even more basically in the reimagined self, with a redirected affectivity and restructured life patterns. Willingness to shift primary commitments at odds with Jesus' way is a recurring theme in early Christian writings. For Origen (died c. 254), restructuring of life had to precede being given the secrets of the Christian way, a matter that for a considerable period meant for some the life-threatening step of resigning from the Roman army. Tertullian (died c. 230) also stresses such basic shifts in ways of living:

> It [penitence and change of one's ways] presses most urgently . . . upon those recruits who have just begun to give ear to the flow of divine discourse, and who, like puppies newly born, creep about uncertainly, with eyes as yet unopened. . . . We are not baptized so that we may cease committing sin but because we have ceased.[29]

So important were these reoriented commitments as prior conditions for admission to full fellowship, the three-year length of the catechumenate was dictated by the usual length of time it took for the redirection of one's life structure.[30]

In the long run, however, the center did not always hold. Though he died three to five decades before either Origen or Tertullian, Irenaeus, bishop of Lyon in Gaul, influenced the shape of theology for centuries. Irenaeus's apologetical treatment of Christianity directed at Greek *thought* had behind it a legitimate academic thrust common to intellectual adherents of all religions.[31] This apologetic thrust, which influenced the Cappadocian and Latin Fathers, eventually became an academic tradition centering on systems of thought, encountering pagan philosophy rather than pagan religious ways. These Fathers looked to non-Christian philosophy for the intellectual means of grasping revelation conceptually. Though never completely overlooked, Christianity as a way of living — encountering concrete symbols and embodying specific practices — tended to be pushed into the background and became in its radical embodiments reserved for the monastic tradition and later for religious congregations. When eventually doctrinal statements came to be the norms of the community's authenticity, the text of the community's own life practice as a radical and indispensable means of interpreting the wider world received less focus. The double text meant to be bound together, the text of Scripture and the text of practice, came to drift apart.

In several places in his writings Farley explores the more recent ways the disjunction of doctrine and practice has been carried into our own time.[32] While the importance of living the gospel has never been lost — that is, the norms for acclaiming "heroic" holiness have always been centered in life practice — the emphasis on practice for more ordinary individuals and communities diminished. It is possible to conceive of religiousness as unconnected or only superficially connected with patterns of life practice, with the consequence that one's "religion" is a matter of the head, not of the hands and feet. Thus, whole regions of human activity can become exempted from gospel norms, such as the way one holds property or uses money; one's employment, its kind and outcomes; or one's exercise of social or political power. A tendency to envisage doctrinal instruction as a sufficient means of incorporating the young into the life of the community might be another contemporary — and fatal — instance of this error. Bureaucratic preoccupation with doctrinal exactness while overlooking antigospel patterns of life might be still another. To those who ask, "Who envisages doctrinal instruction this way?" I point out that we do not so envisage doctrinal instruction in our theory but rather in our expecting religious commitment to emerge from instruction cut off from the lived patterns of discipleship in communities of worship. My students of the early 1960s nimbly leaped to point out that error.

Pieris's analysis of this history is actually getting at Christianity in its character as a way of life, as agape, a way of living out a message of love in concrete practice:

> To say "Jesus is the Word" is not enough; the word must be heard and executed for one to be saved. To say "Jesus is the path" is not enough; one must walk the path to reach the end.... What saves is not the name of Jesus in the hellenistic sense of the term, but the name of Jesus ... in the Hebrew sense of "the reality" that was operative in Jesus.... In fact, the knowledge of the name or title is not expected by the eschatological Judge, but the knowledge of the path is (Matt. 25:37–39 and 44–46).[33]

The kerygma is not a theoretical, logical proposal but a "metalogical proclamation which cannot be demonstrated rationally." Its most convincing proof is witness, the lived-out agapeic behavior of some person or persons. In a passage that challenges all local churches in the way they embody the gospel message, Pieris claims:

> Saying that Jesus is the medium of salvation requires that the ones who say it display the fruits of liberation.... A christology receives its authenticity from a transforming praxis which proves that in the story of Jesus, which continues in his followers, the medium of salvation is operative.[34]

One can communicate the coherent vision of Christian faith to any person who will stay still long enough to hear it. However, the communication of *the way of being a Christian* and the embracing of that way for oneself are quite another matter. Usually the validation of the Christian way is through action — first, the action of those who show that it is possible to live Christianity and that indeed it, as Spirit-filled, does save and, secondly, the action of the one who embraces it for oneself and finds that, yes, for me it is God's gift. Of course, Christianity claims more than this. It claims that its way is also socially salvific, as announced by Jesus in the kingdom of God. That part of the Christian reality is verified in the social action of Christians for a just world.

Multiple implications for pastoral action emerge from these ideas, as we shall see. An obvious one is that the church is a zone where all offer thanks to God, ponder God's message, and also struggle with the problematic of practice.

The Material Conditions of Living

So far I have used various expressions to name the kind of life we live: the material conditions of life, life patterns, life structure. Some readers may have found this use of language unhelpful because it is inexact or vague. I sympathize because I myself have not found a literature laying out the material conditions of life with the specificity I would like. Though Marx's important work on the material bases of life was groundbreaking, it was never worked out with highly specific examples. Possibly the specificity needed can best be attained by particular people struggling to name the patterns they themselves live, first in their own homes and then in their communities of worship and places of work. I have found help in this matter in a few pages of Daniel Levinson's *The Seasons of a Man's Life*, a study of sequential stages in the lives of men.

In examining the transition to early adulthood, those five or six years between eighteen and twenty-three or twenty-four, when a person is moving from the world of adolescence into a first taste of adulthood, Levinson finds young men making a series of choices decisive for the life patterns that will determine much of later life. These somewhat tentative initial decisions lay the foundation on which will be laid a life structure. Speaking specifically of men, Levinson describes the life structure this way:

> By life structure we mean the underlying pattern or design of a person's life at a given time.... A man's life has many components: his occupation, his love relationships, his marriage and family, his relation to himself, his use of solitude, his roles in various social contexts — all the relationships with individuals, groups and institutions that have significance for him.... The concept of life structure — the basic pattern or design of a person's life at a given time — gives us a way of looking at the engagement of the individual in society. It requires us to consider both self and world, and the relationships between them.[35]

Seeking a way to analyze a life structure, Levinson becomes more specific, naming the choices a person makes and how the person deals with their consequences: "The important choices in adult life have to do with work, family, friendships, and love relationships of various kinds, where to live, leisure, involvement in religious, political and community life, immediate and long-term goals."[36]

Here Levinson has moved into descriptive analysis, which lays out patterns easily overlooked. This is a first analytic step. A second step would be critical analysis, by which the life structure is not only described but judged from some other, "outside" vantage point. The only such vantage point Levinson uses is psychological adjustment, that is, whether the person remains tolerably happy in the particular life structure and, if not, whether he can make adjustments. My own critical vantage points are different, entailing the person's contribution to the human good and the life structure's coherence with religious commitments.

Unfortunately Levinson leaves us to work out any more specific descriptive details for ourselves. The task is not a simple one, as I found out in attempting to apply life structure to the brief period of the young-adult transition occurring in the late teens and early twenties. What many young people, both men and women, do not realize is that during the late teens one is in a key phase of establishing one's *ways*. At that time one is developing behavioral patterns and an eventual life structure that will direct one's life for a long time to come: tastes in food, patterns in the use of time, preferences in and even styles of watching TV, ways of being with older people or of avoiding them, ways of behaving in groups, ways of studying, of reading, even of reading the newspaper — or a way of not reading it. It is not that every one of these ways is being newly formed, for indeed many of them go back to childhood. Still, freed from the countervailing childhood pulls from parents and home, a young person easily but unawares cements these ways into place. Being formed at this time are ways of driving a car, ways of using alcohol, ways of talking about and relating to the opposite sex, ways of dealing with the truth, ways of getting one's own will, and, far from the least important, ways of thinking about and using money. Behind the nexus of these patterns is a life structure that affects commitments.

Even these suggestions could be fleshed out in greater concreteness. Some research into rape by young men shows that a relatively high percentage of such rapists are members of athletic teams. Apparently there are ways of talking about women that become patterned in particular groups, such as fraternities or athletic teams, and these ways of talking can reinforce attitudes toward women that lead to rape.[37] On the other hand, there could also be groups of men who in their way of speaking of women exhibit and reinforce attitudes inimical to rape. What I am getting at here are patterns of interaction and of speech. A life structure is a pattern of choices and ways of living, including speech patterns, that become the accepted and eventually the established way for a person. Once set in place, the pattern tends to perdure, in spite of shifts in location, career, or even marriage partner.

For every age group after childhood (though children inhabit life structures too, at first chosen *for* them but eventually chosen *by* them), life structure then says a great deal about the focus of our attention. Evidence of those matters attended to in a particular life structure can be found in specific documents and information of the sort that could be entered into court records. Specifying such documents and facts, as I did at the beginning of the chapter, is meant here to provoke application to specific situations and ways of living. One could do a useful descriptive analysis of the material conditions of one's life by examining patterns of ingesting food, drink, visual/aural information, visual/aural entertainment. What one ingests, as well as where, when, and with whom, might provide the basis of a fruitful analysis. A similar evaluation could be undertaken about one's residence — its size, cost, demand for care, proximity or distance from work, proximity or distance from other family or friends, and so forth. For some people, the costs and other consequences of buying a home set the overall framework for life structure: the income needed, disposable income available, transportation needs, possibilities for leisure, and so forth. I will return to this matter in chapter 5 to explore how society and culture influence these choices and patterns.

"Sacralizing" Life Structure by Refusing to Judge It

As noted previously, the matter of examining and judging life practice is largely ignored in literature of a pastoral nature. Church bureaucracies remain much more troubled by what they consider lapses of orthodoxy than by lapses of orthopraxis.[38] There exist strict procedural norms for the order of ritual. But, except for sexuality, entire areas of life are excluded from gospel norms. In one of his writings, the Renaissance humanist and reformer Erasmus of Rotterdam offers a blistering but comic critique of such blindness to the more important aspects of Christian living in his own time:

It may happen; it often does happen, that the abbot is a fool or a drunkard. He issues an order to the brotherhood in the name of holy obedience. And what will such an order be? An order to be sober? An order to tell no lies? No one of these things. It will be that a brother is not to learn Greek; he is not to seek to instruct himself. He may be a sot. He may go with prostitutes. He may be full of hatred and malice. He may never look inside the Scriptures. No matter. He has not broken any oath. He is an excellent member of the community. While if he disobeys such a command as this from an insolent superior there is stake or dungeon for him instantly.[39]

Again and again in the history of Christianity the sort of question Erasmus raises here about lived discipleship resurfaces. As a social movement affecting European Christians, the Reformation itself is an important instance of such resurfacing.[40]

Once alerted to the dangerous shift in some patristic writings to right understanding as more crucial than right doing, the churches, we might expect, would have greater sympathy for liberation theology's contemporary reemphasis on practice. Yet in the nations of economic privilege and in the churches of the middle and upper classes this reemphasis on practice has not taken place. Why not? One could further ask how it might be possible to move this issue more to the forefront of the agenda of local worshiping assemblies. I seek to pursue these two questions before reflecting on some of the problems I myself see in moving toward greater attention to life structure.

Why then has liberation theology's shift toward practice not assumed greater attention in the churches of privilege? There are many reasons, one of the chief being that in any society some groups are economically privileged by the social institutions. Those in the economically privileged strata find their privileges right and just. Their sense of rightness is reinforced by the social order's meaning system — the society's culture. For what a good human life is like, culture presents a set of norms most easily met by the privileged classes. As products of persons of privilege, those meanings maintain the social order supporting those persons' interests.

One should not be surprised if religious understandings are also enlisted to promote such a social order and the privileges it offers some. Those trained to mediate religious meaning may have sprung from the privileged classes, thus being accustomed from their earliest ages to interpret religion so as not to contradict social class. As a result, the very questions asked here are disallowed as mean-spirited and judgmental. Unwittingly, perhaps, these religious teachers can sacralize social class. If their sacred texts seem to privilege the poor, they may conclude that the true, deeper poverty is not economic misery, which does not afflict them, but emotional deprivation, which may.[41] It can happen that just as the lives of the privileged classes are dramatically different from those of the poor, so the religion of the privileged can be fundamentally reoriented so as to suit their privileges. Thus, the very places where the privileged assemble to worship provide them with a chorus of other voices affirming their status of privilege, in much the same way as do their network of friends and family, neighborhoods, schools, places of business, social services, and so forth.

In response to my second question, "What can be done?" I affirm the situation to be hopeful, for the possibilities of conversion away from a "God for me" to Jesus' "God for the dispossessed" are always latent in any Christian group, because of the ultimate and normative claims the gospel imposes on all. Such normative claims make religion a zone of judgment, evaluative of all reality. If some group's sacred texts in fact privilege the poor as a key locus of the manifestation of God and if they as a group ever embrace this feature as normative for their lives, they will soon find they have to live a religion different from the one typical of churches of the privileged and comfortable. Such a shift will not happen automatically but only from approaching the interpretation of sacred texts from what I will call a "hermeneutics of dislocation." Here the norms of fidelity are not found via self-interest but by crossing over to the needs of those trapped in situations of economic misery and other forms of oppression. Stances of dislocation point to the strangers, to those who first appear to be nonneighbors but come to be seen as the human face of God. Bonds with such neighbors are forged through actions of solidarity. Such actions dislocate the comfortable from their life structure, allowing it to be scrutinized.

And so, since Christianity does privilege the poor, it bears within itself radical possibilities of contesting the excesses of wealth. Here is the answer to my second question of how it is possible to move the question of practice more to the center of worshiping assemblies. This move will never happen easily but only as part of a struggling, step-by-step recovery of a seminal feature of Christianity's own religious understanding. Once any ecclesial group recognizes and embraces the radical or culture-contesting features of its faith, its search for religious coherence will involve a struggle with life practice.

Warnings about Reflection on Life Practice

I have used the term "struggle" to speak of a local church's effort to discern its religious faith's consequences for life practice, and the word implies that the correction of life practice cannot be done by formulaic cut-and-dried patterns settling the matter forever.[42] Indeed, working on life practice is not without problems, three of which I describe briefly here: the need to recognize multiple options among valid choices, the temptation to substitute moralizing for the work of discernment, and the need to accept religion as a zone of judgment.

Jesus' own way of living and his teaching provide the definitive norms for those who would follow him. But since Jesus' preaching shows wide boundaries of what is acceptable discipleship, even here we have no blueprint done to exact scale. Though the norms provide guidance, their nature is to offer general directions within which persons and communities have leeway, depending on circumstances and insight. Thus, the struggle with life practice suggests there are multiple possibilities for answering the gospel call for discipleship.

The process of discernment is an ongoing, indeed endless, feature of discipleship and of discipleship's discourse about life practice. At the core of the problem of becoming more preoccupied with specific patterns of behavior lies the question of how discernment comes to be located at the heart of a community's life. Superficial communication on superficial issues leads to a superficial church. Significant discourse on significant issues of discipleship is the antidote. As we will see in the next chapter, discernment is not the task of leaders only but of the whole local people seeking to make sense of the gospel in particular circumstances. The history of response to any seminal feature of the Christian way reveals the variety of choices that have in fact led to heroic fidelity.

Moralizing, a process by which one person seeks to prescribe behavior for another but from outside the horizon of that other person, is an inappropriate way of fostering the life practice I am advocating here. Moralizing is a lazy way of dealing with the dilemma of specific response to the call of Jesus. Basically nondialogical from a position of assumed power, moralizing offers glib oughts and musts, when what is needed is a grappling with the dilemma of multiple acceptable choices in concrete circumstances. Moralizing's demands are so cheaply made anyone can walk away from them unaffected. Being invited to enter a community of ethical discourse based on normative sacred texts would seem the proper way of engaging people's religious consciousness. What I advocate here are reflection and analysis, not so much about particular acts as about the entire context of living and how particular acts relate to it. Reflection and analysis engage, in a way moralizing cannot, the problem of behavior from the point of view of particular persons and groups in particular circumstances. When a community engages its members in the problematic of behavior — exploring in a particular time and place Jesus' proposals for living — those members will have entered a process they can inhabit as their own, not one pushed on them by religious bosses.[43]

Basically, the process I have in mind is one that embraces the role of judgment in religious traditions. By its nature, a religion is a zone of judgment. This same nature involves it in an endless process of interpretation of situations and events toward judgment and decision. Holding its meanings to be ultimate and salvific — normative — a religion uses those meanings as a yardstick for evaluating all of reality. But norms are not formulas. Persons of good will may prize certain norms over others and arrive at different conclusions deserving respectful dialogue.[44] Also, religious teachings might not touch directly on areas of life that have their own norms, such as aesthetic criteria of beauty in the arts. Still, for religious persons ultimate norms are always there in the background able to be activated when claims conflict about what is truly good or beautiful or just.[45] As already noted, these norms can be subverted by being reduced, usually unwittingly, to legitimations for society's institutions and culture. In such a case religion undergirds, and in a sense verifies, society's unspoken claim that *its* meanings and institution are the ones that are truly ultimate. Religion can still sell its heritage for a bowl of pottage.

Searching for a Method for Reflecting on Practice

Despite many allusions heretofore to specific patterns of life practice, in very few places have I named those patterns. What are some ways of exposing and naming the practices we actually live or of finding alternative practices? What is the religious, historical, and cultural context in which we attempt to so name and expose? Are there methods for exposing the difficult-to-discern features of the life practice lived by the local church or by individual households? Are there any procedures that might be suggested as a way forward in the task I have sought to examine here? The elaboration of such procedures is the further work that follows from the call for more attention to life practice.

As noted earlier in the chapter, there is an absence in pastoral literature — liberation theology excepted — of the question of living practice of discipleship. The absence is not total, nor has it ever been, as shown in the long history of the veneration of those who proved themselves virtuosos in embodying gospel values in their own lives, the saints. There are contemporary authors who deal explicitly with the problem, while others are dealing with questions like inculturation that, if followed through to their logical end, will lead to the matter of life practice.[46] Further, the practice of discipleship is an art not a science, and in art there is no one correct way. Also, "failure" in art is more ambiguous than in science, where, say, an experiment at its completion is either successful or not, but artists scorned in their lifetimes can later be hailed as creative geniuses. If there is any method in art, it is best uncovered in an "after the fact" examination of what actually happened rather than in an a priori statement of theoretical outcomes.[47] Here the appropriate descriptive word may be "process" rather than method. As Marianne Sawicki points out, one learns to do by doing, and by doing justice one has access to the Risen Lord.[48]

Given the historical, religious, and cultural landscape, how do we approach further work on the material conditions of the practice of discipleship? Case studies of local churches that have been able to transform concrete church practice toward a more radical gospel life provide helpful clues about how such a transformation takes place.[49] Marianne Sawicki reminds us the Gospels themselves are such case studies, if we will only allow ourselves to recognize them. My hunch is that any such transformation comes from a kind of "cultural dislocation," a shift from the comfortable assumptions driving church life structure to a series of troubling, problem-filled matters that need attention and a new way of proceeding. These case studies cannot focus only on shifts in the church's inner operations; they must get at how the church responded to gospel challenges in its own social context, especially in its responses to the victims of society, those proxies of Christ in our midst who enable us to "see the Lord."

My one quibble with the capsule case studies in Patrick Brennan's valuable *Parishes That Excel* is that so many of the excellent developments are described at a managerial and programmatic level without sufficient attention to the wider social context in which the church exists.[50] To describe "excellent youth evangelization" in a church ringed by military bases without at the same time probing the church's stance toward the programs of death and domination embodied in those bases does not help get at the sort of life structure conditions I have in mind here. Could a youth evangelization program be named excellent at the same time that it has removed from its Good News Jesus' call for nonviolence or a critique of militarization and weapons production? Could there have been parishes that excelled managerially in Nazi Germany?

Concrete procedures are called for, by which local groups might work toward the sort of cultural dislocation that could lead to transformed life practice at the communal level but also in individual homes and lives. The national- or synod-level staffs of most denominations have set forth such procedures for the local churches. Farley offers an outline of such a procedure in his important, but tightly reasoned, essay "Interpreting Situations."[51] This outline could be concretized and made accessible to many. A similar sort of procedure is offered in the 1984 statement of the Canadian Roman Catholic bishops, *Ethical Choices and Political Challenges.*[52] What they call a "pastoral methodology" for helping the church make judgments about social conditions is as follows:

A. Being present with and listening to the experiences of the poor, the marginalized, the oppressed in our society;

B. Developing a critical analysis of the economic, political, and social structures that cause human suffering;

C. Making judgments in the light of Gospel principles and the social teachings of the Church concerning social values and priorities;

D. Stimulating creative thought and action regarding alternative visions and models for social and economic development; and

E. Acting in solidarity with popular groups in their struggles to transform economic, political, and social structures that cause social and economic injustices.

In my view this process has built into it clear elements of cultural dislocation, via encountering the life situations of the "nonpersons," examining the causes of their misery, making gospel judgments about these situations, and acting in concern with these people as our sisters and brothers in Christ. If a local church embraced these steps, it would at the same time begin the process of its own transformation, not just toward self-denial but also towards a new sensuousness and appreciation of all God's gifts.[53] These steps would send members delving into Scripture in a more attentive and more questioning way.

The verb forms at the start of each step in the proposed methodology suggest the key to finding new forms of religious practice in the church lies in engaging in new, more radical forms of action. In situations where religious practice has become identified exclusively with prayer and worship, members may question whether these actions represent a religious practice at all. The question is important, for the issue is a revisioning of the ministry of the local church and of the proper forms of practice for our time.[54] As I will examine in the following chapter, decisions about such action are not properly made for the community by "leaders." They have to be made by the community via its primal action of speaking.

However we look at them, these forms of practice will continue to provide the meaning of the local church for its members. The teaching taught by the practice is certain to remain more powerful than any kind of teaching that ignores practice.

Questions for Discussion and Reflection

1. Can you think of any instances in which your church's theoretical position is not an actual practice? Give examples. On the other hand, which theoretical positions are most immediately put into practice in the local congregation?

2. What are some of your local congregation's more important manifestations of "teaching represented by the practice"? Has the question, What do we actually stand for? ever been researched in your local congregation?

3. Gutiérrez claims that the very life of the church is a place for doing theological reflection. What would it mean for this principle to be active or implemented in your local church?

4. Do you accept that the church's foundational way of bringing the gospel to others is by means of witness of life? If you do, what does that mean for a local congregation?

5. Can you think of any "false" practices that generate a false theory of what the local church is meant to be?

6. What are the "fruits of liberation" in your own local assembly?

7. Many are intrigued with Levinson's description of the development of a life structure by young people. What does that description say about the life structure of older persons?

8. Does Christianity privilege the poor — or not? What do you say?

Notes toward a Way of Examining Life Structure Elements

In his introduction to *The Archaeology of Knowledge* (New York: Pantheon, 1972, p. 12), Michel Foucault claims that history is not so much found in ideas or what people thought as in documents and in what people specifically did. Foucault is getting at the concrete realities of actual living. If we were to apply this insight to our own lives (or to the clergy of the local congregation), what sorts of documents or information would/might we need?

It is important to note that the matters below are descriptive and preevaluative. They are not easy to face — first, because we are so familiar with them, which convinces us that we already know this information too well and thus the process seems silly, and second, because the eventual reconsideration of these patterns can be threatening.

Becoming Aware of Life Practice

Housing and Necessities

- documents on the size and location of housing (floor plan and property survey), on the costs of this housing and how financed, on the economic arrangements taken to supply the needs of the housing and those living in it

- cash-register receipts or credit-card bills showing the amount spent for food

- bills showing how much was spent on employing those offering services within the house

- documents showing specific information on how much was spent on telephone and other communications services (TV, cable, on-line service; available in common where clergy share housing)

- documents showing the size and condition of individual living quarters

Disposable Income

- credit-card bills

- receipts showing amount spent in restaurants and description of class of these restaurants

- bills and receipts showing amount expended on transportation and the various forms of transportation, for example, automobiles and their make

- receipts or list showing amount spent on books and periodicals, along with their titles

- documentation of the amount put into various "investments:" savings, stocks, bonds, personally owned real estate

- all bills and listing of dates and places for vacations taken

Use of Time

- any appointment books, schedules, and so on detailing the patterns of living within the housing

- descriptions of meals: frequency of meals taken in common, duration of individual and common meals, character of conversation (or televiewing) at these meals

- description of the amount and character of television or videos watched

- description of the films or other entertainment attended

- description of the frequency of moves outside the housing for work (or pastoral) purposes and for other purposes, such as entertainment or shopping

- description of the amount of time spent in reading and the names of the items read

- description of the amount of time spent in study and in preparation of sermons and other professional pastoral interventions/ activities

CHAPTER FOUR

HOW WE SPEAK IN THE CHURCH

As Houseguest or Family Member

HOW DOES IT HAPPEN that adults who can master the speech necessary for dealing competently with the fairly complex matters of nutrition, household and personal finance, child rearing, basic health, cuisine, and so forth — and can give intelligible accounts of these areas to their children — come to be unable to speak of their faith to these same children? This question has nagged me since my years of working full-time with adults in parishes, and I am left wondering about the conditions under which adults who hear talk about faith's mysteries weekly in their churches come to be so religiously inarticulate. Pope John Paul II boldly asked basically the same question in Africa: "How is it that a faith which has truly matured, is deep and firm, does not succeed in expressing itself in a language, in a catechesis, in theological reflection, in prayer, in the liturgy, in art, in the institutions which are truly related to the African soul of your compatriots?"[1] This same question needs to be asked about the religious speech of Christians in the nations of toxic consumerism. If such religious inarticulateness is actually a common feature of many religious people today, then the practice of the local church somehow fosters it in ways too often overlooked. How does it do so?

I wish to expand this question by examining the specific conditions of speaking and listening in local assemblies and the consequences of those conditions. I have already stressed that theology of the local church is often an articulated theory without a corresponding practice, whereas the actual practice of the local church produces an unarticulated "theory" in the form of unspoken and therefore unquestioned assumptions about what it means to come together in the church and about how power is to be exercised there. My underlying conviction is that the potential of the church to be a sign of good news will not be realized unless the conditions of speaking in the local assembly are changed. Local communities seeking fidelity to Jesus could be zones fostering critical discussion about what it means to be wisely human in our day. At present they are generally not and will not become such zones without radical shifts in the ways the people come together and interact. Where the people of a local church exercise little social and cultural agency, it is a sign that the procedures of that local assembly actively, though in many cases unwittingly, foster passivity.[2] The position of "the people" in many local churches is like that of a houseguest, warmly welcomed but made aware of her proper place in the household. Her welcome is connected to a series of unspoken rules: Do not critique the polity of the household by commenting on the parenting practices or the housekeeping skills of the hosts. Enjoy your stay here but know your place — and know, especially, that this is not *your* place. Such unspoken rules demarcate the limits of a houseguest's agency.[3]

In my reflections on the conditions of speech in the local church, I offer two perspectives: the textuality of a religious group, with judgment and critique as normal features of religious coming-together, and speech examined as an exercise of power relations. Then I will examine the conditions of speaking in the early church and the current conditions calling for change in the way discourse is currently done in the local church.

Text, Judgment, and Power in Local Churches

Local Church as a Text

A helpful metaphor for examining the church is "text." Viewed as a social text,[4] the local church is the living out of convictions that inevitably establish concrete, examinable patterns of living. As a visible, accessible text, the life of a group of worshipers is like the life of an individual. Any biography forms a text that can be examined for its integrity and coherence, a fact that might embarrass any of us who ponder the matter deeply. Similarly, religious convictions eventually configure a local corporate reality open to scrutiny. As a text, local church life can be examined in its concrete patterns of action for their coherence (understood as sensible connections between action and conviction), for their integrity (understood as the embeddedness of action in conviction), and for their ability to communicate the group's originating convictions. As a network of observable practices, a local church is, for better or for worse, a way of speaking and acting about the things of

God. Local churches are much more aware that they have sacred texts than that their own living is a text that should, but may not, verify the sacred texts.[5]

Like text, "fabric" may provide another metaphor for the accessible life patterns of the local church. The corporate fabric of the church possesses both texture and pattern. Texture, which gives the feel of a fabric, results from the quality of material used to weave the cloth and the particular way the strands are woven together. Pattern emerges from the design woven out of the material. Texture and pattern can be easily overlooked, though they need not be. Attending to these features is a work of evaluation and, in some cases, appreciation. Actually the corporate fabric of the church is as visible as the architectural patterns that form the church building, though rarely taken are the time and energy necessary to discern these corporate patterns and their meaning.[6] If we decide to recognize the textualness of our corporate life and then examine it, the process will uncover the often neglected question of what sort of text its life should represent.

In the apostolic era the local church saw itself to be an accessible sign of the cheering news announced by Jesus that change to new, more human ways of living is possible. The early communities formed after the resurrection tried to embody such change in the specific ways they shaped their lives. Their togetherness was to be an accessible sign of God's holy commonwealth having taken root and now growing in local soil.[7] In those communities and their way of living, the implications of Jesus' mission was a concrete imagination of an alternative way of being human. At issue was not an idea but the specific realization of a new way of being in the world and of interacting with the world. If New Testament evidence shows these communities were far from perfect, it also shows preoccupation with credible ways of living.

The questions asked in subsequent ages have been, How will we be able to embody Jesus' imagination of human possibilities in the concrete circumstances of the present? How will our gathering in Jesus' name escape the seductions of our society's business-as-usual agenda? Questions such as these echo through the centuries. They were the questions that led the Reformation and Counter-Reformation. The label most frequently pasted onto those who pushed against or contested countergospel social agenda was "heretic." In fact these were reformers working within the faith system and proposing alternative ways of being faithful to the originating deeds and words of the tradition. When their efforts were embraced by the prevailing powers, they were venerated, even as saints; when not, they were verbally disparaged or physically trampled down as evil persons.[8]

Often enough, reformist critiques were not those of single individuals but of small, informal, often spontaneous groups, associations, and communities rooted in "disenchantment with the established order and with canonically recognized forms of community organization, ministry and leadership."[9] Such groups offered ecclesial patterns a dose of creative critique supported by alternative ways actually being lived out by these groups. In general these communities developed structures of participation far greater than found in the established ecclesial order. The activity of such persons and groups was an active work of interpretation, of pointing out the distance between the way of living of Jesus himself and of his disciples and those of a particular age.

Reformers and reformist communities alerted others not just to the conditions of life within the church but also and especially to the wider societal and cultural conditions in which the church existed and which shaped its own life patterns. To use current language to name their activity, they used a religious social hermeneutics to interpret what was happening around them. In thirteenth-century Italy, Francis saw the dangers of the new market economy emerging in the towns, with its promise of wealth for the few. He and his followers lived out a radical alternative. The very regularity of these reformers in history represents the inevitability of critique in a faith rooted in normative accounts of its roots. Indeed, the ability to critique and judge is a normal part of any religion, and even more so for efforts to be faithful to the patterns of Jesus' life practice. This is one reason why various strategies to silence religious critique are never fully successful.

Religion as Zone of Judgment, Active or Suppressed

All religions claim ultimacy for their meanings, in the sense these interpretations of the world and the deeds they call for are considered the key to a truly human life. These understandings are awarded a place of priority in the scheme of meaning, providing the grounding purpose out of which one lives one's life and finds one's place in a religious "chorus." For their adherents, these understandings measure what is humanly salvific or liberating. They measure the true from the false, the real from the illusory, the authentic from the fake, and even good from evil. Such meanings, already interpretations of reality, become a field of further active interpretation of reality. By their nature — a nature open to being subverted — religious groups are hermeneutical communities.

If we accept, for example, that all persons are temples of the living God, that view will ground a way of interpreting those situations imperiling human dignity. If God's call to side with the poor, to abjure violence, or to work for the social practice of justice becomes our call, it changes the way we approach reality.

My point here is simply that religious norms are like all norms; they give rise to judgments about value, about goodness, about rightness — about reality. However, religious meanings as ultimate lend a special edge to judgments based on them, what we might call "the edge of ultimacy." Could religious judgment be muted or stifled, either permanently or in certain situations? If so, what are the conditions under which this "normal" activity ceases? How did the Franciscan commitment to poverty come to be compromised so relatively soon after the death of Francis?[10] Is this what happened in the Christian churches of Germany that capitulated to national socialism or in those of the United States that so devoutly endorsed the 1991 U.S. war against Iraq?

Critique appears to be normal and even inevitable where communities are actively struggling with the implications of their own norms, but not all communities are willing to engage that struggle. One way that critique is short-circuited is through the very patterns of speaking in the community. Local churches — or the local gatherings of any religion — can split over time into two unequal groups: those who possess religious agency as producers of religious insight and those who lack it as consumers of the insights of others. When this division is in place in local churches, critique can either die or be deadened for at least two reasons.

First, if religious leaders, set up as agents among the passive recipients, falter in their fidelity to the originating religious ethos, the entire community of dependency also falters. Leaders can transform religious conviction into categories that do not contest or contradict the wider social conventions. Those who produce religious insight can tailor it like a suit of clothes to fit the dimensions of the wider society. The fabric of religious conviction is cut down to accommodate the proportions of the wider culture in what is often a stunning fit. Such tailoring doubles the elite status of religious leaders, whose skills with religious fabric can be well-appreciated by the wider nonreligious community. Historical examples of such faltering among leaders, both clerical and lay, abound.

Secondly, the very forms used to direct the coming together of the elites and "their people" can render the people mute. The people become accustomed to being without voice, being told what to think, how to apply their sacred texts, when to respond with their affirmations of what is said to and for them. The resulting silence has a character very different from the engaged quality of contemplative silence. In considering the parable of the seed (Matt. 13:4–9), where the seed falls on rocky soil, takes no root, and withers, one might ask whether the conditions under which this parable was remembered and recorded had to do, not with individual stoniness, but with the social conditions of communal life hostile to the natural fecundity of what was sown (see Matt. 13:20–21; Mark 4:16–17). When forms of nonagent participation characterize worship, one might ponder the possibilities of worship's infertility. "Worship" is a word brimming with connotations of agency. When it is used to name a communal activity suppressing the agency of the community, "worship" helps hide the fact of passive participation. Nothing very deep is questioned by the elite speakers, and nothing spoken by the elites is questioned by their audience. Whatever insight exists within the assembly has been dulled by norms of nonagent silence.

This description may seem like a generalization, and so it is. But its generalizing feature describes the particulars of the coming together of many local churches. The particular conditions of speaking are set up in such a way that only some speak, becoming the ones who tell the others what they should think and do. Under such conditions, not admitted to exist, the interpretive community as a community of discourse is not permitted to exist or dares not permit itself to function. A gay friend from New York City tells why Roman Catholic gays will not tolerate opportunities to speak in open exchange at worship. In his view, such exchanges threaten to raise serious questions about gay lifestyles that gays themselves do not want raised, let alone pondered. He mentioned specifically two matters: overconcern about (and overspending on) fashion and the issue of permanent commitments. The preset, measured responses of the liturgy serve to keep these religious issues buried, to the comfort of all, but fundamentally contradict liturgy as the action of the people; here it is the inaction of the people.[11] Could there be in every congregation such lifestyle/life-structure issues that cannot be engaged except by some process of public struggling with the relevance of sacred texts to our current patterns of living?[12]

Another reason the rules of speaking in local churches can come to reflect such passiveness is, I suspect, that those who set up these rules and those who obey them are not used to thinking of speech situations in terms of the use of power. There are ways of approaching speech situations that suppress questions of power and others that surface them.

Speech Situations as the Exercise of Power

Approaching speech situations from the angle of linguistic critique offers results different from approaching such situations from the angle of social critique. Linguistic analysis in the idiom of Saussure looks at grammatical correctness, at the relations among symbolic elements in speech, and at the meaning produced. Competence is found in the correct use of these symbolic elements, which, abstracted from their social context, are considered autonomous. Social analysis of speech examines a different series of issues, for in place of grammaticalness it looks at acceptability, a social question. In place of language (or langue) as normative in itself, it looks at the legitimacy of language and its appropriateness to a social context. In place of the relations among symbolic linguistic elements, it chooses to probe relations of symbolic power among speakers. In such social analysis the issue of meaning is put within the context of issues of value and power. Instead of looking at a speaker's competence in manipulating the elements of speech, social analysis examines the speaker's position in the social structure. Instead of viewing a speech situation only as understanding abstracted from social relations, the social critique makes language an instrument of action and use of power. In other words, relations of legitimacy, of acceptability, of symbolic power, look at language as a form of social practice in particular situations, with power relations brought to the fore. Such social power relations have implications for discourse in the local church.

By studying the social conditions that make language's production and circulation communally possible instead of the logical conditions that make language semantically possible, Pierre Bourdieu calls attention to the concrete circumstances in which speakers have different social roles based on power, with some being producers of speech and others consumers. In his own words,

> practical competence in the use of language is learnt *in situations*, in practice: what is learnt is, inextricably, the practical mastery of language and the practical mastery of situations which enable one to produce the adequate speech in a given situation. The expressive intent, the way of actualizing it, and the conditions

of its actualization are indissociable.... [I]n practice, [language] production is always embedded in the field of reception.[13]

Apart from their roles as abstractions in dictionaries, signs have no existence except in specific patterns of linguistic production. These patterns of production are always embedded in power relations.

Two speakers with equal command of grammar and syntax speak to each other. If the first has the power of greater authority, that power determines in part the speaker's role with regard to the second speaker, giving the first more "say." But there is another kind of power — linguistic power. If the second speaker has a greater command of language, say, a greater mastery of rhetorical skills, then this fact somewhat offsets the authority-power of the first speaker and may even override it. Instead of more say, the second speaker has better say.[14] Bourdieu insists any science of discourse adequate to real situations must lay out the laws specifying who may speak, to whom, and how. At meetings of religious-education professors, feminists have helped many become aware of these patterns by noting publicly the ratio of women to men present and the ratio of women to men who make interventions. Writing about speech situations in the local church rarely adverts to such laws or the social situations grounding them.[15]

One could work out an educational theory about the place of discourse in the church — and still not advert to the uses of power in the assembly, including the power of the educator. The power of the educator is not dealt with as power but assumed to be benign and liberative. An educational theory or program that effectively takes for granted the participation of any person or group of persons in the educative process — especially children — colludes in hiding this question of power. This is all the more true for those Christian education programs awarding themselves liberative titles. An overlooked feature of all Paulo Freire's work in situations of oppression is that he never takes participation for granted; it is always problematized and dealt with by means of various kinds of negotiation. Not all who invoke Freire's name implement this aspect of his work.[16]

The textuality of the local church, especially its patterns of speech, are features needing special scrutiny in our time. These patterns can mute the normal work of interpretation and judgment that should characterize communities following texts held both ultimate and normative. If so, these patterns must be changed.

The Call for Change

Out of the many ways of approaching the need for change in the speech conditions of the local church I opt for two: the practice of the New Testament communities and the need for deeper structures of participation in contemporary life. In taking this tack, I am choosing to leap over many centuries when forms of imposed silence seemed not to obstruct a living faith. The complex historical record of these years, once retrieved, needs sophisticated analysis to get at the positive and negative sides of church practice and at the social conditions fostering religious life.[17]

Authority in the New Testament Churches

Recovering a simple account of the use of authority in the earliest Christian communities is impossible.[18] Spread across various regions, the communities were marked as much by their idiosyncrasy as by their commonality.[19] Amid this variety, commonalities surface, including the following noted by David Power in his essay on authority in the early church. The key authority is Jesus, whose words and deeds were marked with the authority of God's own hand, and who continues to exercise that authority as Risen Lord. Any other authority comes from its association with Jesus' Spirit and the gifts of that Spirit. Paul is an example of one whose authority arises from the power given him by the Risen Lord but is *verified* in part by Paul's link with the apostolic tradition and by his ability to foster fidelity to that tradition within the wider church. Clearly Paul's gifts were for the community and prized in the light of their value for the community. This last way of putting the matter shows authority primarily located in the community of faith and its corporate life of fidelity, rather than in any individual. The power of the Risen Lord was found in communities that adhered to the apostolic word. Their own fidelity was what made these communities zones of judgment able to decide whether particular conduct or belief represented fidelity to the Risen Jesus. Structures and office existed for maintaining the communion-in-faithfulness among members and not for the enhancement of leaders.

The postapostolic formation of a fixed canon of scriptures and of a common rule of faith accepted by all the communities did not, then, arise in a vacuum. The context of these developments was concern that God's grace and power mark the living reality of the eschatological people. This was the same context of the evolution of the episcopacy. The church's own life patterns were to give evidence of the authoritative apostolic word. The role of the bishop was to foster that same witness by being a radical part of it. Often enough it was the most radical (male) witness to the community who was named bishop: "Bishops...needed to corroborate the witness of their teaching by the witness of the power of the spirit in their own lives."[20] They did not see themselves as the sole exercisers of authority but, on the contrary, as called to recognize and affirm the Spirit's power in persons with no ecclesial office. In such a self-understanding, the apostolic tradition, i.e., scrutinized fidelity to Jesus-faith, holds prior place over office, not the office prior place over tradition.[21]

Sad to say, this arrangement did not last as episcopal authority gradually swelled. What also grew was a diminishment of gifts and a neglect of the charismatic authority of ordinary believers, especially after the fourth century, contradicting New Testament evidence that a commonplace of earlier church life was a recognition of divine power at work among various members of the community. The manifestations of divine power in members of the community came to be neglected by leaders, and, as Power puts it, "pushed to the margins and into legends,"[22] such as those about wonder-working saints.

As I read Power's historical survey, I become aware of how seldom anyone in any worshiping community of my memory has been singled out and noted for holiness or for gospel wisdom or for an unerring, gospel-based sensitivity to and healing for those who suffer. One might surmise that the single norm for being among the worshipers has to do, not with the way one lives one's life, but rather with one's ability to be quiet. As often as not, encomiums for members of the local church are not about goodness or holiness but have been reserved for those in the highest ranks of authority and those who have donated the largest sums of money. Alertness to signs of the Spirit of Jesus in the community has been swallowed up by alertness to the powers of office or of wealth. The exception is communities vowed to gospel poverty, such as religious orders and groups like the Catholic Worker, where attention is regularly called to the power of God in exemplars of Jesus' way.[23] David Power is getting at the loss of a seminal aspect of our tradition in the current life of the churches. Near the end of his essay, he asks, "Could it be that the most vital factor for a reconceptualization of power and authority in today's church will be the development of a genuine sensitivity to the presence and work of the Spirit among all the faithful, so that it may serve as an ecclesial, rather than an individual, criterion of true faith and apostolic community?"[24] As this statement suggests, what is at issue is power, the use of administrative power to free the deep religious power of people alive with the Spirit. History suggests the power of a religious people can career out of control unless harnessed by conduits of love and reflectiveness — by the judgments of an enspirited community. This "reconceptualization of power and authority" is what is behind my writing this chapter, with its focus on the enspiriting power of human speech among the people who gather in the name of God.[25]

Restoring the Assembly

Many denominations seem to be struggling with the question asked both in the academy and the wider society: Whose voices shall be heard?[26] In the following section I will offer some reasons why this question is so crucial today. Among Roman Catholics, as in other denominations, liturgical renewal is a focal zone of efforts to foster deeper and truer participation. Worship is to be orchestrated in such a way that the service itself invites intelligent participation. As set forth by Vatican Council II, this renewal goes under the name of restoring the liturgical assembly. However, these efforts cannot succeed if the participation question is limited to the zone of worship alone.

Those who first used this language of "assembly" to speak of the people gathered for worship may not have fully understood its implications. "Assembly" is a word with quite different connotations and implications from another word that might have been selected to describe the people at worship: "audience." The audience are those who listen; they attend to the words of others; usually their "word" is in the form of response of a particular kind: appreciation. In some usage, audiences are to be entertained. "Assembly" is a very different kind of word. It bristles with the political implications of speech as an exercise of power and of the back-and-forth of discourse about the use of power. As a political unit, the assembly, which at least among Roman Catholics died out centuries ago, involved more than the ritually proper responses at worship. Naming the gathering for worship an "assembly" does not produce the reality signified by this word, though it does problematize what happens during that gathering.[27]

Liturgical reform cannot succeed as the rearranging of various elements within the framework of worship alone. Looking at the liturgy as a framed picture and reform as rearranging figures within that picture misunderstands the scope of the problem of restoring the assembly. Restoring the vernacular, reconfiguring how the people relate to the altar and the presider, expanding liturgical ministries, and restructuring the lectionary are doubtless necessary, but insufficient. Because the key matters are not in the picture but in the horizon that contextualizes the picture itself, those shifts do not succeed in restoring the assembly. Certainly there are people in the picture, but they neither consider themselves an assembly nor function as one. Restoring in any deep way the political dimension of how we come together calls for more than updated liturgical choreography; it will involve fundamental changes in the way each person conceives of the self as an agent in an agent-full assembly. For a community this self-understanding will not come from being preached to about agency but from transformation in the way people come together and act in their togetherness. How might such a transformation affect the assembly of worship?

An agent-full assembly is one where power of action is situated squarely in the people, but not as an audience responding to the words and actions of the ones with the real agency, the presider and those who direct song. Composer and liturgist Bob Hurd writes,

> Needless to say, if those with leadership roles (presiders, musicians, readers, and so forth) exercise them in...distorted ways ..., the rest of the community will exercise its role in a correspondingly distorted fashion. Vatican II's profound call for the active participation of the people tends to be realized in the form of an audience that is attentive rather than inattentive, that dutifully makes token verbal responses instead of remaining silent.... Unlike the talk show or the concert hall, there is [meant to be] no audience, not even a very intelligent and attentive one, in the reformed liturgy.[28]

In his essay Hurd implies but does not spell out how crucial to the creation of a sense of assembly are all the other ways of coming together in the community and how speech functions within them. Refiguring speech within the liturgical frame depends on its being refigured in all the linguistic exchanges outside that frame. All these ways, I claim, ritualize power relations, often in unspoken but effective ways.

"All speech situations are defined, not so much by the things said as by the things that cannot be said."[29] How finances are handled, how conflict is resolved, how surveys and "consultations" shape (or do not shape) policy, how opened or closed to scrutiny are decisions, how learning is structured — all these ways provide the context that either belies or verifies a local community as an assembly. Major ways of subverting empowering speech that might forge an assembly can be found in policies that are "none of your business," space whose use cannot be questioned publicly, and monetary policies reserved for the scrutiny of small elite groups.

Curiously, Hurd does not offer ways of allowing a freer flow of speech within worship itself, even though the restoration of an assembly may not be able to proceed without restructured speech. I once heard a well-known liturgiologist advocate in impromptu remarks such a freer flow, though I have never seen the point in his writings. He questioned whether in a time of electronic communications any group of people can tolerate the passivity — incessant statements about the power of the Word of God notwithstanding — of three readings followed by a homily. When I heard this question, I found myself asking what would shift in the conditions of speech in worship if at the end of the service, the readings for the following week were announced or even distributed and worshipers agreed to reflect and pray over these readings during the week, in preparation for the following week's assembly. Then during the next assembly, after the reading of these texts, the assembly — at least those wishing to do so — would break into small groups of three or four and listen briefly to one another's response to these readings. Such a procedure would signal that all can speak, that all can respond to the Word of God, that all can learn from all, that the Word of God is on the lips of the people. After this sharing, the presider could invite a certain number of persons to tell of some insight heard from another so that the group would have some sense of common and uncommon issues. Finally, the presider might make a very brief comment summarizing some feature of the insights from the floor. What might in the beginning be a somewhat messy procedure might in the end find the Word of God alive within the assembly.

Even this thought is laced with problems. How would a group know they are ready for such a procedure? How would they go about deciding? Will the community agree to such a procedure, and if they do, will they allow for those who will not want to participate in the procedure? The shift in the conditions of discourse I have in mind here cannot be achieved by mandated procedures imposed on an unwilling community. Mandated procedures arbitrarily imposed by power have been the cause of the passivity I am seeking to expose. I suspect true participation is possible only when people may opt without recrimination for legitimate marginal participation, which makes way "for the unconstraint that encourages all human flourishing."[30] Rather than arguing against the tradition-laden practice of preaching, I instead ask for deeper reflection on the conditions of preaching and their consequences. Whatever changes emerge will do so over time, and then with groups ready for them or moving through them one step at a time.

The possible designs are endless. I know of a local church where twenty-two groups of about fifteen persons each meet weekly to discuss the implications for their individual and corporate lives of the readings for the coming Sunday. On Saturday morning, representatives from each group and anyone else wishing to attend meet with the presider for two hours to discuss the insights of the group dialogues and how these insights affect their community of worship, city, nation, and world. The presider prepares a homily for the assembly in the light of these insights. The following Saturday, the first agendum deals with how faithfully the presider dealt with the Word of God the previous Sunday. These optional groups (called "base communities") first began over twenty-five years ago as a gradual work of formation that in time came to involve significant numbers of the community.

Restoring Judgment

Forming base communities and similar uncomplicated procedures may help reshape the conditions of speaking and relocate the sources of wisdom in the church at large. Without denigrating the role of the presider, such approaches put the work of interpretation into the mouths of the people. Further, the role of judgment, which is normal in a religious body, comes to function as an ordinary part of the people's coming together. However, in the face of endless historical examples of inauthentic judgments made by various churches, one may ask how these judgments will themselves be kept open to the gospel mandate.

The problem of exercising a gospel judgment may not be simply one of paying close attention to Scripture and then asking what our response should be in the light of revelation. The deeper problem may be that we bring to the sacred text itself prior — and sometimes unacknowledged — commitments that shape what we find in Scripture or limit its being applied in certain circumstances. For example, consumerist capitalism fosters the conviction that the use of one's earnings is entirely a private matter. Individual and family finances are "none of anyone else's business," an attitude already suggested in reference to church finances. Not speaking about personal finances in public is a convention reinforced via various seldom-named customs. U.S. males are quick to reveal to one another what work they do but are not socially permitted to ask one another impolite questions about what salary they earn. In talk about "hard-earned money," the "hard-earned" part can be explicated, but not the "money" part. How we think of and use money is just one example of areas of life that can be excluded from public or even quasi-public speech. These exclusions are in place prior to and usually after encountering the sacred text.

Whatever commitments we have to the sacred text are modified by prior commitments that go to make up a stance. "Stance" is a way of positioning oneself that shapes one's encounter with some reality or issue. Political theologians raise the issue of stance when they question the significance of prior commitments for the interpretation of faith itself.[31] The reason Christians of different denominations sometimes find they have more in common with members of other denominations than with some in their own is, I presume, they share with these others a gospel stance they do not share with many in their own denomination.

Stanley Hauerwas holds that decisions alone cannot account for our moral life. Behind decisions is what he calls a "narrative," a life story embodying factors we might be unable to name but that together forge our character and the commitments that go to make up character. The standard approach to understanding ethical action finds this notion of narrative too subjective. In Hauerwas's view, in the end we all tend to choose moral appeals to the patterns or fabric of our actual lives, simply because

> our experiences always come in the form of narratives that can be checked against themselves as well as against others' experiences. I cannot make my behavior mean anything I want it to mean, for I have learned to understand my life from the stories I have learned from others.... An agent cannot make his [sic] behavior mean anything he wants, since at the very least it must make sense within his own story, as well as be compatible with the narrative embodied in the language he uses. All our notions are narrative-dependent, including the notion of rationality.[32]

Much of the writing on the church as a hermeneutical community ends by focusing on how such stances, given various names, influence our interpretation of anything, including our sacred texts.[33] Most of this writing points out that the work of interpretation must at some point make decisions about what is essential in Christian faith today and what is not. In order to make nuanced judgments about the faith priorities needed today (i.e., judgments about stances), communal interpretation must often go beyond uncovering a tradition already present in the community's identity and propose matters never before considered.[34] One of the stances Francis Schüssler Fiorenza and others propose is solidarity with the suffering. This stance will not allow us to justify the status quo in society but will instead question and critique it — not so much as individuals but as a community of fidelity empowered to speak.[35] In the end, any move in the directions I have only hinted at here will be messy, if not disruptive. Skills at conflict resolution will hold as much weight as those of interpretation.[36]

The Crisis of Participation and the Importance of Agency

There are reasons why participation, while not a new issue, is being felt today as a matter of new urgency. Joshua Meyrowitz offers cogent reasons why this may be so. He suggests that over the past thirty years electronic communications have altered for many people their own sense of their proper place in the scheme of things. Television especially has disrupted the isolation of whole groups of people by putting them in touch with a common pool of information and perceptions: "By merging discrete communities of discourse, television has made nearly every topic and issue a valid subject of interest and concern for virtually every member of the public."[37]

The prestige once offered elites depended on their being only occasionally available in onstage behaviors, and then in carefully crafted front-stage events. Most of their more ordinary behavior occurred backstage and out of view. Behaviors once clearly "backstage" and hidden behind closed doors are now opened to public scrutiny, ceasing thereby to be worthy of awe or even of respect. Such scrutiny, of course, demythologizes the elites' front-stage behaviors, as when Richard Nixon's backstage office conversations were via electronic magic made accessible to all. When a camera can zoom in on someone's blowing his or her nose front stage, some of the intended glamour of carefully crafted appearances will erode. A nationally prominent lawmaker awaiting a presidential State of the Union message to Congress is caught by the TV camera letting his eyes roam the ceiling of the chamber in which he is seated. The hint of inebriation suggested by his unfocused eyes and his seemingly flushed face may become, in the consciousness of televiewers, vaguely attached to a question of whether he in fact does drink too much and whether he deserves the power he wields. Thus television can foster a process of demystification, reducing the images and thus the prestige of leaders. According to Meyrowitz's analysis, the result of these shifts is a greater sense of one's relationship to the whole and of one's place in it. One no longer wants to stay in one's so-called proper place. What has shifted is the politics of participation. One could argue that a similar shift took place at the time of the Reformation, when literacy gave many a new sense of their right to read and interpret religious meaning.

Whatever the merits of Meyrowitz's analysis, the fact remains that some churches are in a crisis of membership in the sense of a radical nonparticipation, while others are in the midst of dramatic new patterns of involvement. In Ireland today there is a struggle going on between the two patterns. The locations of mandated involvement are hemorrhaging, as in weekly participation in the Eucharist, especially among the young, while parishes and non-parish-based groups grounded in discourse and searching for a humanizing form of living are prospering. In traditionally Catholic Quebec a similar and well-documented shift has already taken place.[38]

Base community, house church, core group, fellowship groups — however they be named — such groups are offering alternatives to consumptive muteness. Of greatest service to "leaders" in such groups are skills of the ear, not those of the tongue and mouth; skills of discernment more than those of planning and management; skills of inviting questions rather than doling out answers. Systemic nonparticipation appears to be less and less tenable today.[39]

The crisis of participation within the churches, to repeat Meyrowitz's position, is part of a much wider social shift of our time. Meyrowitz's analysis does not mean that all people are becoming aware of, in the critical sense of "understanding," how power is used or are utilizing committed stances from which to make judgments. Meyrowitz notes simply that they want a say and are shifting their own relation to leaders and, to a certain extent, events. Still, Meyrowitz is getting at newly emerging questions about personal and social agency in a time when there appears to have been dramatic reductions in such agency. While I obviously believe Meyrowitz is correct, my suspicion is that the drive toward agency is fundamentally ambivalent. Those who want greater social participation fear it as well, and their drive for inclusion is countered by a drive for avoidance. They fear the time and energy greater involvement will cost. It will surely disrupt patterns of passive entertainment. Religious participation is also afflicted by its own fears of too-great involvement and even of religious transformation that greater participation may call for. Such fears can be actual while unacknowledged. Pastoral people do well to be aware of them.

The issue of agency threads its way through much writing in a time when so many find themselves reduced to being cultural consumers, objects of the action of others. One could say it is a major theme of our century. A few of the many authors who have written on this matter from various angles are Maurice Blondel (1893), Charles Sanders Peirce, John Macmurray, Hannah Arendt, Raymond Williams, Paulo Freire, Jürgen Habermas, Alain Touraine, Stanley Aronowitz, Henry Giroux, Francis Schüssler Fiorenza, Paul Ricoeur[40] — and almost all feminist writers. In a time of the managed consciousness, agency as an issue is not going to disappear.

Throughout these pages and from multiple angles, I have emphasized the agency of individuals and communities as crucial for church renewal. Yet, to understand agency from a Christian point of view, a fundamental point must be clear: the deepest agency is God's.[41] For Christic imagination, God's agency must be internalized both conceptually and imaginally. Søren Kierkegaard's analysis of preaching helps uncover the imaginal ways we construe God's agency,[42] and it does so using an analogy reminiscent of Meyrowitz's clever onstage/offstage/backstage analogies. Kierkegaard implies that most people see the church by means of a theater analogy. In this analogy the preacher is the actor, and the congregation is the audience of theatergoers. God is prompter, with the correct script, whispering the correct lines to guide the actor. Those in the congregation (theatergoers) sit and pass judgment on the actor's performance, possibly being moved by it. However, Kierkegaard proposed a corrective analogy for a more fruitful understanding of ecclesial agency. In his proposal, the prompter is not God but the preacher, directing all her attention to the actor. The actor is not the preacher but actually a corporate person, the congregation, who act out the plot or narrative. But Kierkegaard has not forgotten the audience. The audience is God, "the critical theatergoer," witnessing the performance of the actors aided by the prompter. God's presence is decisive.

In this final section I want call attention to two powerful warnings about the erosion of agency in a time of electronic communications, plus the claim of a French thinker that we are entering a new time, which is calling for a new and different kind of agency. The first warning is by Ben Bagdikian, a media analyst concerned about the greater and greater control of international communications by a smaller and smaller group of companies, all controlled by males. Since attention is a significant religious issue, the implications of Bagdikian's following concern for "the harvesting of attention" should concern religious people:

> One of the most profitable commodities in the modern world is human attention. Whoever can harvest it in wholesale quantities can make money in kind. In the United States, one Nielsen rating point reflects 1 percent of the country's 90 million television households. One percentage point for a network in prime-time audience share represents more than $30 million in added revenues each year. Nothing in human experience has prepared men, women, and children for the modern television techniques of fixing human attention and creating the uncritical mood required to sell goods, many of which are marginal at best to human needs.[43]

Similarly, social critic Stanley Aronowitz writes of the way electronic communications can colonize the social space — including the judgment — of vast numbers of persons:

> [I]n the last half of the twentieth century, the degree to which mass audience culture has colonized the social space available to the ordinary person for reading, discussions, and critical thought must be counted as the major event of social history in our time. Television, film, and photography, far from making culture democratic, have fostered the wide dissemination of industrialized entertainment so that the capacity of persons to produce their own culture in the widest meaning of the term has become restricted.[44]

The word "colonize" might well signal deep alarm among those with religious sensitivities, let alone religious commitments. What is being colonized are the spirits of persons we all know. Communities of religious discourse can possibly, but not easily, free these spirits toward a deeper humanization.

According to Alain Touraine, the French social theorist, many twentieth-century social movements have functioned as totalizing thought systems that effectively reduce human agency.[45] When people become consumers of a movement's ideology and allow themselves to be massed into groups, they become objects, not subjects. They find their collective identities within a fixed representation of society.

Touraine's point is not that people should act only as individuals or monads but that the social struggles in the future will be over symbolic products and over who will represent society to itself and in what way. More and more social action will be about the cultural model on which social life is constructed. Feminists lead the way in this work.[46] The managed consciousness dependent on mechanisms of engineered change will be replaced by agents active in defending local liberties against technocracy in its various forms.

In rereading Touraine I have come to see how the questions I raise in this chapter illustrate the positions he spells out in his writing. What this means is not that the questions point to "in" ideas but rather that the tensions within Christian church groupings are part of larger social questions of our time. What one of Touraine's commentators called "the reconstruction of a representation of social life" is what so many of the thinkers I have cited here are working at.

Conclusion

Whether we like the fact or not, our communities are held together not just by symbols and doctrines but also by practices. The cogency of all three is not self-maintaining. A community's meanings can perdure as vital realities only if its members work in these meanings, chewing them over, to get at both what they signify in themselves and their implications for present circumstances. Practice, understood as the implementation of belief in particular circumstances, enlivens meaning.[47] The community examines whether its response to the world squares with its beliefs. Such examination and response cannot happen without dialogue, intense conversation, about what the community's sacred texts mean in its social circumstances at the local and wider-than-local levels.[48] Rebecca Chopp reminds us the move to dialogue is not automatic or easy:

> The theological turn I argue for [changing the values and hidden rules that run through present linguistic practices, social codes, and psychic orderings] envisions the purpose and nature of the church as a community constituted through and for its proclamation to the world. Such a revisioning of the church, a reconstructed logic of the *ecclesia*, is an exceedingly difficult task, since despite the desires for community in modern theology, it is

quite clear that conditions for any substantive sense of community are far from us.[49]

Without denigrating the legitimate role of preaching in a local church, one could say the problem in the churches both is and is not a problem about preaching. The problem *is not* preaching in the sense of our needing more stimulating pulpit proclaimers; it *is* preaching in the sense that the voice from the pulpit can still all other voices. Enlivening speech cannot always be one-way, from elites who know the right interpretation of the tradition for this current circumstance to the congregation that passively ingests these insights. Such one-way communication does not maintain the community's faith, if only because the dilemmas of current circumstances are not the problems of elites but of the entire community as an interpretive body seeking faith's implications for these particular circumstances. The issue here is communion, not the pseudocommunion of physical proximity but the deeper communion of the shared Spirit of Jesus, a shared spirit rooted in deeds and words. Enlivened by the struggle for insight, the community embraces action as a corporate entity and enriches the public life of the wider society, where common action rooted in discourse is so badly needed.

My own hunch is that the issue underlying common speech toward common action in the assembly is that of mutual formation. Without speaking to one another of our struggles toward gospel fidelity, there will be lagging fidelity. Lacking such speech about struggles, the field of the local church tends to be an arid one. I have in mind common speech about the community's struggles and individuals' struggles toward discipleship. The fact and importance of such speech is not unknown. Many parents, for example, are quite ready to talk with other parents of their struggles to be good parents. That speech about their problems, uncertainties, and insights has not only a deep character of realness, but it leads to reflectiveness about parenting and better practice. The religious speech I am describing is likewise rooted in uncertainty, struggles, and a desire for better fidelity. The letters of holy people like Simone Weil and Flannery O'Connor are filled with this discourse of struggling uncertainty. In print I have found such discourse often in Robert Hovda's "Amen Corner" in *Worship* and in varied other places, such as an interview in which Daniel Berrigan spoke of his blankness at prayer. I myself have had such conversations with one or two bishops, with many Xaverian Brothers, with members of the Catholic Worker, with women and men friends, and with all members of a house church. In many religious settings, this formative speech is generally avoided, replaced with talk about managerial concerns. Can it assume its place as a common feature of discipleship?

At the end of these reflections, I find myself asking whether my concerns here are too narrowly Roman Catholic. Would my examples, say, of participation within worship, particularly the Eucharist, persist if Roman Catholics had a strong tradition of ongoing adult catechesis, as do some Protestant denominations, such as the Presbyterians, Baptists, and Lutherans? Would not the corrective of a participatory liberationist catechesis make for the sort of full participation in a community of judgment I have in mind? Where Protestant churches have such a tradition, do the sorts of questions raised here lose their edge? Possibly. I must leave this question open, best answerable by checking the actual practice of local churches.[50]

However, from casual conversations with leaders in various denominations, I find the crisis of participation marks almost all denominations in the United States and that it is not solved by one-dimensional strategies. The problem is not exclusively Roman Catholic or educational. The centuries-old systemic silencing can be corrected by a systemic loosening of tongues. Such a loosening will affect the character of all ecclesial life, including worship. In the face of much writing about the influence of catechesis on worship, I have here tried to deal with how the conditions of worship can have a stultifying effect on the overall ministry of the Word and all other aspects of living out the gospel message. The struggle to become a community of judgment and action inevitably alters the context of worship, the character of worship, and even the ritual itself. It establishes a new rule for the household of faith: "Guest no longer; now a true member of the beloved community."

Questions for Discussion and Reflection

The Material Conditions of Speaking: Questions about Procedures

1. What procedures are in place, or could be in place, to encourage the congregation's members of all ages to talk out (informally and/or formally) their religious questions, issues, convictions?

2. What procedures will lead to a local church policy that reflects the view of the people as an assembly?

3. How will decisions of small groups, such as committees, be submitted to the assembly for reflection, questioning, modification, and/or ratification?

4. Are there any categories of matters affecting the life of the church that are not but should be put before the assembly for approval?

5. What are the procedures by which minority positions — including dissenting positions — will be heard and recorded?

6. What are the procedures for surfacing and acknowledging that the assembly is divided on a particular issue?

7. What are the procedures for trying to resolve or come to some minimum agreement on these issues?

8. What are the procedures for resolving conflict within the assembly?

9. Are there any procedures in place for directing and evaluating the preaching at Sunday Eucharist? What procedures for feedback from the community would preachers find helpful?

Questions about Attitudes

1. How do clergy view themselves in relation to the speech of the community:

   • As the voice of the assembly?

   • As a voice within the assembly?

   • As the facilitator of the varied voices within the assembly?

   • As a facilitator helping the assembly discover its common judgment?

2. How do those others who serve on church committees or who have appointed ministries within the church view themselves?

   • As privileged voices?

   • As facilitators of the voices of others?

   For example, do those ministering to youth view themselves as those who speak to and for the young or as those who help the young speak for themselves? Is the speaking done in a gospel-centered or gospel-struggling voice?

In programs for adults, how do facilitators see their role?

- As the primary speakers?
- As facilitators of the speech of others?

Regardless of what these persons say, how are they perceived?

3. How often and in what ways does the community itself express its corporate voice on its own convictions?

CHAPTER FIVE

LIFE STRUCTURE, OR THE MATERIAL CONDITIONS OF LIVING

An Ecclesial Task

GUSTAVO GUTIÉRREZ's groundbreaking *Theology of Liberation* explains the seminal character that *practice* has in any authentic account of Christian faith. Practice is a special problem today that may be put as follows: What we actually live we do not name as part of our religious fidelity, and what we name as religious we may not live in our daily life patterns. The significance of our embeddedness in a concrete life structure is often overlooked, partly because we prefer to understand our religious practice as ritual practice or prayer practice, not life practice. So stated, this problem is one of religious incoherence. Can this pattern be reversed so that what we actually live we can name, examine, and, if need be, change in the light of our tradition? Can what we ritualize as our guiding religious principles actually guide us in structuring our daily living? What are the conditions under which life patterns can become a matter of religious reflection? Behind these questions is the conviction at the heart of this book: that the teaching represented by actual practice is more powerful and formative than the teaching stated but not practiced.

To be frank, though I have probed these questions from various angles in the previous pages, I am unable to offer a formula for answering them. I am unsure of the actual procedures by which a particular religious group might deal with the issue of life structure. The something that must be done occurs in a particular time and place, involving particular people with particular habits of thought and patterns of living. It is a gospel response, not to a generalized world, but to a specific, particularized one. After giving, sometimes far from home, a public talk about some pastoral issue, I am occasionally sought out by someone from the audience, who lays out a difficult problem in her local church or diocese and asks me to reflect on it. Most often my response is a reminder that the problem arises in a particular situation and the solution must arise also in that same situation. Hence, my advice is, "Pay attention to the particulars of the problem and look there for the particulars of the solution."

Hovering in the shadows of any such advice are real dangers, all having to do with replacing reflection and wise hesitation with moralizing and cut-and-dried formulas. One of the problems facing all Christian denominations is the attempt of opposing sides to impose behavioral absolutes on each other. Gospel proposals cannot be imposed from without; they must be embraced from within, not just from within the self but from within a community and for most of us, even then, one step at a time, tentatively feeling our way. Even close-knit communities may not agree on specific lines of response and action. The best way of proposing a line of action to anyone is not via the "shoulds" and "musts" of imperatives but via provocative descriptions of a particular situation, of the various ways it may be interpreted, and of what options we face in responding to it. This would be especially true of the open-ended sorts of proposals and invitations we find in the Gospels. What I advise, and what I myself set out to do in this chapter, is describe rather than prescribe, propose rather than impose.

Discerning Our Hearts and Actions

Those interested in the question of concrete religious practice would do well to consider an essay by James Atlas written for the *Atlantic Monthly* in 1984. Atlas lays out for his readers how market-research analysts at the Stanford Research Institute (SRI) in California were able in the late 1970s to decode the purchasing habits of households, thereby providing vital information to marketeers. Using what they named the "VALS typology," analysts were able to divide the U.S. population into nine lifestyles or types, which were themselves grouped into four broader categories based on people's self-images, aspirations, and the products they used. "VALS," the name given this research design and the uses to which it was put, stands for "values and lifestyles program."

On first reading Atlas's account of VALS-based marketing, I was struck by the acute specificity of what the program set out to describe: the particular ways people had of conceiving their place in the world and the concrete patterns of buying that reinforced that place. At that time, my own writing about youth ministry was claiming the churches were overlooking the specific patterns of behavior in which youth tended to be involved. I found most proposals about ministry to youth to be disembodied and idealistic, ignoring the concrete behaviors of youth in speech and action. Atlas's essay signaled to me that what the churches chose to ignore the marketing people were examining with a well-focused stare. My proposal for youth ministry was to assist the young in considering what they may be inscribing in their own lives.[1] Here I carry that proposal forward for other groups.

In the late 1960s, SRI's analysts had started developing marketing strategies for a generation with negative attitudes towards ostentatious consumerism and money itself as a measure of a person's life. These researchers sought to discern the "patterns of the heart" of the new generation, discovering thereby how to anticipate and then satisfy their needs. As a mid-'70s SRI report put the task:

> The central problem in advertising will be how to sell to values increasingly geared to processes, not things. Sales appeals directed toward the values of individualism, experimentalism, person-centeredness, direct experience, and some forms of pleasure and escape will need to tap intangibles — human relationships, feelings, dreams, and hopes — rather than tangible things or explicit actions.[2]

Since people's values influence their spending habits, marketing must appeal to these values.

As a way of indicating just how specific the SRI research was, I will briefly outline the categories into which these analysts cast the U.S. population. All those surveyed were grouped into four general categories, and each of these was broken down into subgroups according to more specific lifestyle behaviors (see the overview on p. 104). These categories become more interesting if we keep in mind that we can find our very own selves located somewhere in them.

The *Needs-Driven* is the first of the four categories, and it incorporates the nation's marginal classes into two hand-to-mouth lifestyle subgroups: the *Survivors* (those able to get by and still maintain a certain dignity) and the *Sustainers* (a "seedy assortment" of ethnically mixed gamblers and touts). This category with its two subgroups represents 11 percent of the U.S. population.

The second category, the *Outer-Directed*, comprising by far the largest proportion of the population (68 percent), embraces three different lifestyle patterns. The first lifestyle subgroup is the *Belongers*, strongly traditional and conformist, who make up the largest single one of the nine subgroups in the VALS typology (38 percent). To quote a VALS promotion: "They get a job and they stick with it; they find a product they like and they stick with that." The second Outer-Directed subgroup is the *Emulators*, who represent 10 percent of the population. They yearn to be achievers but basically do not know how; they tend to spend money on the assumption their ship is still going to come in. The third lifestyle group, the *Achievers*, composes 20 percent of the population. This financially secure group is self-assured and able to exhibit gracious but savvy behavior in varied situations. They are knowing — about their own place in the social order and even about their own drivenness. Marketing appeals must attend to their savvy, self-assured character.

Constituting 19 percent of the population is a third category, the *Inner-Directed*, who fall into three lifestyle groups. The *I-Am-Me* group tends to be somewhat angry, rebellious, and maladjusted. Individuals in this group are bent on "doing their own thing," even if it might mean they could be misjudged in the process. The *Experientials* are a wholesome group seeking "highs" from jogging and other fitness activities, like backpacking, and are inclined toward holistic medicine and yoga. Together these two lifestyle groups make up 8 percent of the population. Making up 11 percent of the population, the third Inner-Directed group, the *Societally Conscious*, are aware of social issues and involve themselves in politics. Concerned about the environment, justice, and the misuse of power for self-interest, their inner-directed energy, while coming from self-awareness, is focused outward. Self-centered marketing does not appeal to them.

The last category, coinciding with a single lifestyle group, the *Integrated*, represents 2 percent of the population. This group represents the VALS ideal: at the same time creative and prosperous. Examples offered are writers and artists who also run lucrative retail businesses. In VALS literature and video promotional material, examples abound of what people in each of these lifestyles are actually like: what work they are likely to be engaged in and how they will probably spend money. This last is, of course, the whole point: the implications of lifestyle and attitude for marketing products. As James Atlas's final words put the matter:

The "bottom line," according to the VALS introductory brochure, is "how to apply values and lifestyle information in marketing, planning, product development, and other areas of business" — in other words how to get across the message that it's okay to be a consumer again.[3]

In his commonsense language, Atlas is describing what Jürgen Habermas calls the "colonization of the lifeworld" by the marketeers.[4]

My own interest in the SRI VALS research is for its careful scrutiny of the behavioral implications of attitudes about the world and how one is to be in the world. These researchers understand that attitudes get acted out in decisions about purchasing. According to Atlas the most recent VALS research probes the connection between sociogeographical location and predictable buying patterns. Indeed, one of the data managers at SRI asked Atlas for his zip code. Upon hearing it, she told Atlas he lived on the Upper West Side of Manhattan and fell into

---

Overview of the VALS Typology

Category 1: *The Needs-Driven* (11% of U.S. population)

- Needs-driven subgroup A: *Survivors* To get by with dignity

- Needs-driven subgroup B: *Sustainers* To get by

Category 2: *The Outer-Directed* (68% of U.S. population)

- Outer-directed subgroup A: *Belongers* (38% – largest subgroup)

- Outer-directed subgroup B: *Emulators* (10%)

- Outer-directed subgroup C: *Achievers* (20% – most affluent subgroup)

Category 3: *The Inner-Directed* (19% of U.S. population)

- Inner-directed subgroup A: *I-Am-Me* (subgroups A and B make up 8%)

- Inner-directed subgroup B: *Experientials*

- Inner-directed subgroup C: *Societally Conscious* (11%)

Category 4: *The Integrated* (2%): The VALS ideal, creative and prosperous

the *Bohemian Mix* classification. Based on his zip code, she could have given him a printout of his attitudes, probable household inventory, leisure-time activities, media habits, and consumption patterns for over seven hundred categories. This manager's claim puts an ironic spin on an ancient prayer Jesus himself must have often recited: "Yahweh, you examine me and know me; you know if I am standing or sitting; you read my thoughts from far away; whether I walk or lie down, you are watching; you know every detail of my conduct" (Ps. 139). While the marketeers have indeed examined us and know us, we ourselves can easily overlook the religious implications of the very patterns they have studied.

Consumer Research and Religious Commitment

On first exposure to the VALS research, some have trouble seeing its religious significance. Yet, for the way it examines the relationship of "affect" and attitude — spiritual realities — to the enactment of particular lives, VALS research gives religious people much to consider. Some churches identify spirituality with ways of praying and worshiping, thereby excusing inattention to the wider configuration of attitude and commitment found in the behavioral patterns of daily life.[5] A whole side of life is implicitly declared off-limits to religious consideration and reconsideration. One passes into prayer and worship through the gate of intention, even when the intention is marginal, whereas one may enter a social location and the attitudes that go with it casually, gradually, and often without attention, not to mention intention.

My proposal is that social location must also pass through the religious gate of intention. Persons unaware of the patterns they have inscribed into their lives might be shocked to learn marketeers can analyze their behavioral patterns by means of a zip code. Put another way, they might be surprised to find out how cleverly market researchers have cultivated sophisticated measures of the specific patterns of their lives,[6] with the express purpose of influencing what their hearts will long for. The patterns of behavior that determine the wider configuration of spirit are what I prefer to call the "material conditions of living." For people to work at being religious without considering the influence of these material conditions on our own human spirits is to "disembody" religiousness, making it instead thoughts about thoughts.

The point of departure for fundamental theology is the way of life mediated by the Christian community. Because that way of life makes its faith-life intelligible and credible or not,[7] the community cannot afford to overlook the specifics of its "way." For local churches to be believable exemplars of Jesus' way, they may have to find ways of reflecting on their practice, not just a fantasy of "praxis," but on the concrete, specific patterns of living among their members and what these patterns mean in the light of their normative texts. By means of communal discourse, these patterns can be brought through the gate of reflection, evaluation, and intention. As strong as the consumerist impetus behind the VALS research, the religious impetus for reflecting on it from an alternative position, using alternative values, is stronger — or potentially stronger. Needed for this task are conceptual tools for understanding and evaluating practice.

Bourdieu's Examination of Habitus

In seeking tools for understanding practice, I turn once more to the writing of Pierre Bourdieu, the French social thinker, for clues to how and why people inscribe in their lives patterns of acting of which they are little aware. Though his writing is subtle and sometimes obscure, Bourdieu offers conceptual tools for naming important features of our lives, and for that reason, he remains inscribed in my list of "conceptual saints." Some have asked whether Bourdieu's ideas might be better grasped in a study of socialization, such as Peter Berger and Thomas Luckmann's *Social Construction of Reality*. Though Bourdieu's work certainly falls within the area of socialization, he has different emphases. Bourdieu's focus is on "practice," meaning what people actually live and what is in some ways beyond knowledge. It was my search for a better way of understanding practices and how they are formed that turned me to Bourdieu's ideas.

Bourdieu is interested in the social conditions that influence people to think and act in particular ways. He boldly states that every economic system successfully produces in its people the inner traits needed by that system.[8] His claim is about all people in a society, including religious people. Coming from a concern with religious formation fostered by congregations of religious practice, I immediately presumed he was wrong because I thought the production of religious attitudes would be either deeper or more powerful — and those attitudes would at least question the values of an economic system. Though he never uses the term, Bourdieu is talking about habits of the heart and attitudes of the spirit that make up what I would call a "spirituality." I was reluctant to admit an economic system could shape the spirits of people formed to put God before any and all systems. However, the more I looked into Bourdieu's evidence for his claim, the more I could understand the conditions under which one's zip code might expose self-inscribed life patterns. Understanding these conditions may help discern counterconditions allowing disciples of Jesus to work toward a conscious embodiment of an intentional, possibly alternative, set of dispositions and life patterns.

Much of Bourdieu's social theory focuses, not on explicit norms guiding social behavior, but on the more subtle production of practices standing outside of rational calculation while entering deeply but unspokenly into behavior.[9] I believe the struggle to master Bourdieu's unfamiliar categories is worth the effort because he provides a language by which to name and speak of unnoticed life patterns. Even if Bourdieu's terminology eventually comes to be surpassed, it will have opened the way to better-honed, more useful terminology.

For Bourdieu, two histories intersect in each person. One is the *habitat*, or objectified history, accumulated over time in objects like machines, buildings, monuments, books, theories, customs, law, and so forth. The second is the *habitus*, the embodied history, a matrix of perceptions, appreciations, and actions functioning as a kind of law written into each person's life from early upbringing.[10] A habitus steeps a person in durable patterns of perceiving, thinking, and acting that are generally outside awareness but fixed in place by objective conditions of living, and perduring even after these conditions change. My translation: You can take the boy or girl out of the mall, but it is not so easy to take the mall out of the boy or girl. Bourdieu sees habitus as not just a series of social practices but rather the "feel for the total game" of a particular culture that is behind one's ability to enter totally the play of that game, focused on moves and next steps, all the while operating within game rules. Though unwritten in any book, these rules are well mastered. One does not think about the game reflexively; one just plays it.

Most of us regularly observe such game playing. I listen to groups of people not well known to each other search for some common ground for their casual conversations. Often, almost inevitably, that ground is found in talk about money and its uses: the recent "buy-of-a-lifetime," the rising prices of such-and-such, tales of "should have bought" and "am going to buy" and "always buy." This is what bubbles up in the flow of speakable concerns spoken out of a habitus structured by consumer capitalism. Unspoken rules let it happen. According to Bourdieu, to be in the game is to be so involved following internalized rules, one does not need to think about rules; one *does* the game. There is a choreography to life's dance that is neither genetic nor written down. Instead it is cultural, learned by being in a particular place and time and among particular people. To repeat: habitus is both outcome and cause, producing the practices that come from playing the game.[11]

Doxa (Greek "opinion") is the word Bourdieu uses for the matrix of culturally induced but unspoken assumptions that become embodied in practices. Practiced belief is more a state of the body than a state of mind. The preverbal taking-for-granted of a particular world as if it were *the* world is what Bourdieu means by doxa. The doxa tell us, "This is how things really are." The child is the exemplar for doxa because for the child enacted belief is instilled in the body itself and in bodily actions as a living memory pad. Social necessity becomes part of nature by being converted into motor schemes and bodily automatisms. For example, an urban child does not just live in the city; the child becomes urban in a thousand ways never brought to awareness. Her urban sense rides on rules of thumb, practical metaphors, and turns of phrase that have been mastered and made productive, generating skillful living in the city.[12] And yet, doxa function in the same prereflective way for the prosperous, self-aware, articulate Integrateds of the Stanford VALS research. In their new homes with their ever-larger closets for their ever-growing wardrobes, consumerist attitudes take on embodied ways of living a life. Robert Coles was onto doxa in his contrasting descriptions of the churches of the rich and the poor (see p. 19). As we shall see, doxa, powerful when unspoken, can be named and brought to awareness.

Bourdieu's emphasis on the bodiliness of a habitus is sometimes underscored by his use of religious language to suggest an almost religious ineffableness to a habitus. The habitus, like God, is beyond speech and is "made body" through a "transubstantiation" achieved by hidden, implicit modes of persuading and teaching.[13] However, when I consider the habitus of an ecclesial body, called by some "the mystical body of Christ," I find its very nature is meant to be explicit or at least to have within it a tension towards explicitness and intentionality. In fact, a religious habitus is the opposite of ineffable: it cannot be maintained as vital without human speech aimed at examining it in the light of the community's never fully integrated meanings. The religious habitus is meant to be questioned, probed, sized up for adequacy, bothered about.

A religious habitus is like the refined skill of the woman walking across a tightrope. She certainly has a practiced, embodied skill, but it is very different, and its maintenance very different, from the casual sauntering of the middle-aged man making his way down a street. The sauntering is like Bourdieu's habitus, not the high-wire walking. Religious practice, even when unfaithful to core elements of its own values, tends to pass through the gate of intention and considerable discourse before it can function.[14] *Faithful* religious practice, like the skill of the high-wire walker, is not automatically self-maintaining; it must be practiced in the sense of rehearsed and worked at. It is always in process. The religious problem Bourdieu exposes for me is religion's aping of the social habitus, sauntering along with it mindlessly, suppressing in the process the radical implications of religion's own beliefs. The uproar Jesus created in the synagogue at Nazareth in his Lucan "inaugural" sermon came from his naming the distance of their actual practice from the sacred texts they claimed to follow.

Once, when I was the religion department chair of a new Roman Catholic high school in Brooklyn, the principal asked me to represent him at a meeting of high school personnel called by an Irish-American pastor of a large parish. The pastor was concerned whether the loyalties inspired by the various high schools were working against students' loyalties to the local church, specifically his parish. His question, which I considered significant, was "Is the school supporting the parish?" The man had affably designed the discussion to be over drinks in his study, a process that loosened his tongue as the time wore on. What came tumbling out as he talked about "his" parish betrayed his own serious racism — particularly regarding Afro-American families moving into dominantly white neighborhoods.

At the time, I was teaching a minicourse on the gospel and racial justice and grappling daily with intense overt racism bubbling out of my student groups. Not as angry and verbally vicious as some of my students, this pastor had the same basic mindset. What he said could have been said by any racist adult in East Flatbush. He represented, not the gospel norm of communion, but the norms of his class, race, and area, and his words turned his own question on its head. Was the school supporting the parish — in these racist attitudes as they existed in the rectory of the parish? No. Overtly and consciously the school was confronting attitudes that seemed to be part of the parish. I wondered if the preaching on Sunday might be supporting in subtle ways the racism I was confronting in my students. What would happen at the Eucharist if I raised in the assembly the issues I raised in class?

My example here is about speech — in my classes, in that rectory, and in the pastor's church — but habitus's deepest level functions beyond speech. Cultural schemes embodied in a habitus pass, according to Bourdieu, "from practice to practice without ever going through discourse" or "attaining the level of discourse."[15] For anyone even dimly aware of how many features of institutional life — of a household, a school, a church — pass into practice without going through discourse, or what I call the "gate of intention," Bourdieu's claim will ring bells. Even more important is his insistence that such schemes cannot leave practice *except* by going through discourse. Though practices that arose in one social context can linger on inappropriately and outside of discourse in a later context — racist ways of speaking are one example — they will not be changed except by talk about the practice itself. This was the main point of the preceding chapter. Of the instances currently abounding in the Christian churches, gender discrimination is one practice currently being dragged kicking and screaming back through the gate of intention.

For my purposes here, another feature of Bourdieu's theory needs to be noted: his insistence that the social orchestration of attitude and action is "conductorless." Since the functioning of the social and economic order is the agent at work, there is no conspiracy on any individual's part to instill these attitudes. It is human to dance, but the choreography of this particular dance is determined socially. Habitus is not a matter of individual influences. In his view, interpersonal relations are only apparently *individual-to-individual* relationships. Socially created by their past and present place in the social structure, people's dispositions are so many indications of their social position.[16] Obviously not all those of the same class have the same "experiences," but they are far more likely than members of another class to be involved in similar situations, as is evidenced in statistical patterns affecting employment rates, income curves, educational attainments, number of paid vacation days, and even the kind of food eaten and the way meals are taken. These patterns shape a social environment with a particular character or "physiognomy" and with its own sense of reality.[17] Such patterns have religious import, as when identification with persons of similar income blinds religious people to the needs of those of lower financial status or produces renditions of the tradition that justify class-based ideology. I for one have had my fill of theology that overlooks the existence and power of the social.

One might ask, Do we lack all self-direction; are we trapped? Is

Bourdieu offering us a totalizing vision of how culture and social position shape dispositions and life practice? Such is not his purpose. His descriptions of socially taken-for-granted practices make for greater reflectiveness about our own place in social systems. His work is potentially liberative, in the sense that understanding social process is a first step in talking back to it.

Possibilities of Contestation

Bourdieu shows how the subjective necessity of the commonsense world is made valid by wordless affirmation, by being taken for granted: "What is essential *goes without saying because it comes without saying* [emphasis his]."[18] But there is another side of this principle: What can be made explicit is able to disrupt what is taken for granted. In other words, when the social world's character as a natural phenomenon is questioned or in some other way brought to awareness, its seemingly natural or conventional character begins to dissolve. What keep habitus in place are assumptions, or doxa, which are actually opinions whose power is maintained by being widely assumed. Bourdieu points out the obvious way of interrupting this pattern:

> The critique which brings the undiscussed into discussion, the unformulated into formulation, has as the condition of its possibility objective crisis, which, in breaking the immediate fit between the subjective structures and the objective structures, destroys self-evidence practically.[19]

To some readers this explanation itself will seem so self-evident that it is not worth exploring. I dwell on it so religious people may see the need for bringing taken-for-granted practices into active religious reflection. Such a discourse is a "natural" part of a religious tradition built on sacred texts, though this naturalness can be subverted.

Because of the perils they regularly face, socially dominated groups possess an interest in exposing the arbitrariness of the doxa. Such perils do not automatically bring these persons to awareness of or speech about their domination and its arbitrariness. For the oppressed to have a "say" about unspoken opinion, or doxa, they need the tools of critical discourse. Critical discourse involves "the symbolic means of rejecting the definition of the real . . . imposed on them through logical structures reproducing the social structures."[20] If doxa are assumed values needing to be made explicit, "orthodoxy" consists of named values that can stand the test of explicitness. In a deep way, religious traditions have the potential symbolic resources for such critical discourse, though these resources are often unused or underused. The potential resources of the Christian tradition for critical reflection are as powerful as those of any tradition.[21] Under what conditions will they become active in the local church?

Religion, Norms, and Judgment

The resources I have in mind are those built into the Christian tradition's use of judgment. As a human faculty perpetually in a process of formation, judgment calls for the application of norms and principles to behaviors, events, situations, and even objects. In my sense here, judgment is active, not passive. It is not done *for* a person or a community; the person and the community are the agents themselves, the seminal point that lies behind this entire book. Norms, no matter how they are used, prompt judgment. Implicit norms prompt implicit judgment; explicit norms, explicit judgment. The VALS research cited above focuses on implicit judgments connected to lifestyle and seeks to manipulate them while maintaining their implicitness. My concern is with explicit norms.[22] As one's norms become better understood and as one gives better focused attention to matters being examined, judgment becomes more skillful, more nuanced, more appreciative, but also appropriately able to point out harmful or inadequate features of what is being judged. This is as true for judging film as it is for appreciating baseball. But the matter is even more complex since norms themselves need to be judged, to assure they are adequate.

Those who work with the young encounter the transformation of behavior that takes place as a young person begins to apply norms to attitudes and actions that had previously drifted along in the implicit currents created by the group. It can happen, for example, that some persons between the ages of eighteen and twenty-two come to a kind of crisis of friendship that involves the selection of new friends based on a new sense of the self and of the sort of behavior judged appropriate to a self more aware of what one stands for. Friends that seemed appropriate at fourteen may not always seem suitable at twenty, when one may have opted for new norms for one's own behavior and that of others. The old taken-for-granted norms, the basis for former judgments, have been examined, found inadequate, and replaced with new ones. The process is not one of disdaining others but of one's judgment growing more nuanced, more skillful, and more discerning.

People who dwell within a religious tradition encounter a set of norms found in sacred texts and in a religious people's history and, for Christians, embodied in Jesus. This seemingly obvious point has striking implications. Christianity, as founded on sacred texts disclosing Jesus' paradigmatic life, is of its very nature a normative, interpretive activity. The interpretation runs in two directions: the community interprets the text, but that same normative text also interprets the community.[23] By means of this back-and-forth of interpretation, the community becomes the text of yesterday brought to fruition today. Skill in applying these norms is a practical art developed gradually over time. No one develops a practical art by hearing over a loudspeaker directions meant to be slavishly applied; the process is more thoroughly dialogical and discursive than that. A religion, however, does not just possess norms; it claims a special status for its norms — the status of ultimacy. These norms are worth living for and dying for. They are seen as humanly liberative and salvific and ready to stand the test of liberative practice.[24] Those who actually embrace religious norms find their lives anchored in judgments based on these norms. Where religious norms are suppressed or not allowed to enter the kind of discourse needed to bring norms to life, something of religion's core is eviscerated. Examples abound in the Christian tradition.

However, if a religion's normative meanings are lived and worked at, they become configured into an imagination of what makes for a good human life: wisdom. This is especially true in a religion like Christianity, which is rooted in a relationship with a specific human person, Jesus of Nazareth, who stood on the side of the "little ones" and whose Spirit is believed to be present in his followers. Religious judgment is both appreciative and discerning — able to applaud what fosters the human but able also to discern good from bad, valuable from meretricious. Religious wisdom knows also the place of tentative judgment when either norms or the situations being judged are unclear. Similarly, it grasps the value of stating judgments in ways that foster dialogue with other points of view.

I stress here the normal, inevitable relation between norms and judgment in any area of life.[25] From a secular or religious point of view, norms engage judgment as a natural outcome of standards. In my twenties I began to read books about the art of filmmaking. As I came to understand some of the principles of the art of film, movies I had formerly liked came to be uninteresting or even distasteful, while others, once considered boring, became fascinating. I am not claiming to have become a film expert based on four or five books. What happened was this: I entered a process of reflecting on what I saw in the light of principles, values, and norms previously unrecognized. This process of engaging judgment is a never-ending one and can involve any area of life, from baseball and basket weaving to international finance and global communications — or to the life practices of religious people in their separate households as well as in their corporate household of faith, the ecclesia. Indeed, an area of life religious people do well to bring under normative scrutiny and evaluation is life structure.[26] Like Bourdieu's habitus, the concept of life structure offers an additional conceptual tool for the sort of reflection on life practice I have in mind. Life structure helps concretize the unspoken habitus of Bourdieu.

Life Structure

Yale psychologist Daniel Levinson used the term "life structure" to name developmental patterns he found in a small, selective sample of men he studied over a period of twenty years (see p. 64).[27] Whatever the limitations of the sample population used by Levinson, his insights are valuable. They show how the dreams and choices of young men in their late teens and early twenties work to establish eventually an underlying pattern or design to each person's life.

Life structure's shaping of life is fixed by a series of decisions taken incrementally over a period of years. Choices made in the late teens and early twenties slowly but inexorably set in place a life pattern. Levinson's choice of the term "life structure" rather than "lifestyle" is worth noting. "Lifestyle" suggests an option selected as a kind of surface glaze to one's life, like the wallpaper selected for a particular room or the fashion style adopted for some occasion. "Life structure" suggests a fixed apparatus, as stubbornly rooted as a tree stump in one's yard.[28] Once in place the structure tends to direct a person's life during early and middle adulthood, a period of over thirty-five years. The word "tends" is important here because life structure is open to being shifted or changed, though not easily, through the same process of decision that put it in place originally. However, there is this difference: many of these decisions originating a life structure are what I will call "decisive-unintentional" because while they are indeed made, they are made casually, without forethought to their longer-term consequences.

It may take some years, for example, for a person to become aware that a decision was indeed made but was not given adequate consideration when made.

Levinson gives attention to friends because of the influence friends have on a range of other decisions. As seen above, my interest in this feature of life structure comes from observing it surface in some young people for early conscious attention and reconsideration — and possible restructuring. A young person may, for example, come to recognize in himself or herself a destructive pattern of behavior, not necessarily a general pattern but possibly one that exhibits itself only when with particular friends. This realization may spark a crisis of friendship, and the person may decide to search for new friends, more in keeping with who one wants to be.

For Levinson, the key decisions affecting life structure have to do with occupation, marriage partner, size of family, engagement in a network of relationships with extended family and friends, plus a wide range of interactions with society and its institutions that take place in one's leisure time. Here I find concreteness walking hand in hand with vagueness. In the end Levinson has left the specification and analysis of life structure up to us, by implicitly inviting us to work out the nuances for ourselves. The fact of a pattern or structure shaping our spirits is my concern here. Can we bring it from the wings, where unseen it directs our actions, to the front of the stage, where it may stand disclosed in full light?

There is a difference between the habitus explained by Bourdieu and the life structure outlined by Levinson. The doxa, or unspoken assumptions, behind a habitus are so deeply embedded in a way of living they *cannot* be spoken without being somehow disrupted. Levinson's life structure, however, is theoretically nameable or "sayable" but generally unacknowledged in its significance for the way one lives a life. When a habitus remains unnamed, and thus in place, and a life structure remains unexamined, and thus not open to restructuring, the material conditions of actual living persist beyond the reach of interpretation, including of course, religious interpretation. However, the Christian tradition has a long history of concern about the implications of behavior for religious fidelity, as seen in the well-documented catechumenal process of reflection on and possible restructuring of behavior as a necessary condition for baptism and full ecclesial membership. To be sure, this tradition also embraces periods when emphasis on behavior was wrongheaded, mistaking peripheral elements for core ones, thus displacing the core. The Reformation sought to correct just such errors. Abundant examples before and after the Reformation show how cheap moralizing replaced an integral communal discourse about behavior faithful to the Jesus tradition.

The life practice of individuals is found in the size and locale of their dwellings; the way they eat and drink, including what and when; their work, including the time needed to get to and from work and the conveyance(s) used; what they do with their leisure time; what they read and what they are paying attention to by means of their reading; what films they see and what they watch on television; and the way they think about and use money. These activities become patterned in what I am calling "practices," and these practices shape people's lives, what their spirits are all about, what some of us would call "spirituality."

These material conditions of living affect not only the common people in the church but also their leaders, as an overseas student powerfully suggested. We had been speaking of the scourge of un-employment among the young in his country, Ireland, and I had asked whether the Roman Catholic Church was concerned about the prob-lem. What collective action had the college of bishops taken? He claimed they were not concerned. In explaining why not, he gave the following account:

> To understand why the problem doesn't engage them, you have to get other information. Find out where the various Irish bishops take their meals. Find out who joins the bishop at his at-home meals and how often. When they eat outside their residence, with whom do they eat and who pays the bill? You may find out that almost never do these men eat with unemployed youth. They eat with an entirely different, almost opposite, social class. And when they eat fancy, wealth pays the bill. By and large the people they eat with are the same ones responsible for the policies creat-ing youth unemployment. And that's why not all the bishops are concerned with unemployed youth.

Whatever this account's accuracy, it fascinated me in the way it fo-cused sharply on the material conditions of the religious leaders' eating patterns and how such conditions structure the consciousness and the actual practice of the ministry of those leaders. The opposite of what I call "cheap moralizing," these largely descriptive comments surfaced questions about patterns of behavior. Lacking attention to the life structure of all members, including clergy, efforts to reimagine and restructure congregational practice will, I fear, be insufficient, if not illusory.

At the local church level, life structure embraces a similar range of patterned activities. The way the community comes together, the voices heard, the voices heeded, the personages celebrated in the community, the persons whose numbers are dialed or whose doors are approached by the staff, the way the community's physical resources are used, the style of living of those who serve the community, the kinds of issues that arise in homilies, the ways (or lack of them) to respond to these issues — these are just some of the matters needing interpretive scrutiny. Asking questions such as the following is one way of uncovering a local church's life structure. On what occasions or in what circumstances in the past year has recourse to power outside the community, say, to the law or the police, been taken and why? Does the church have investments, a portfolio? What is in it? A commitment of the community's money to some project or company is, to put it drolly, a commitment backed by money. I for one have never once heard the issue of investments problematized for individual members of any congregation I have attended, nor have I heard raised the issue of the congregation's own corporate investments. The peace-activist slogan intoned ironically "Pray for peace; pay for war" highlights this ambiguous sign value of money. As C. Ellis Nelson reminded us years ago, the very arrangement of buildings on a church property is itself sacramental of its priorities.[29] Such tangible arrangements can belie the stated commitments of the church. This problem of being what we say we are, though a perennial challenge of the church, is the particular sticking point for disciples in a culture of illusion.

The Community of Interpretation

If language is a structuring device of all consciousness and the condition for the meaningful existence of all other practices, then the inability to speak of the fit, or lack of it, between our life patterns and what the gospel calls us to is itself a definitive practice. Until this practice of nondiscourse is disrupted, no change is possible. Even should some catastrophe disrupt the present practice, all will see the resulting shifts as temporary disruptions and await the moment for restoring the old, unexamined patterns of practice.

The practice of a local religious group is always a text able to be examined for its coherence, or lack of it, with the community's own sacred writings. As such a text, the community's practice produces either a radical religious intervention in the world or a domesticated or safe one. The radical intervention measures the world's structures by the community's sacred writings. The domesticated intervention accepts social structures and the meaning system that supports them and fits the sacred writings into those structures. The community's life is a version of the social order but in religious guise. French social philosopher Julia Kristeva claims that religiousness in its semiotic, uncontrolled pole offers the possibility of a radical subversion of social reality. But she also notes that organized religion can undercut that subversive, questioning element, in effect, subverting the subversion.[30] If religious people merely repeat religious formulae, without letting them intersect with their life practices, then religion can be just another practice of the dominant culture. I myself doubt a local church can engage the question of gospel fidelity in our time without becoming at its core a community of interpretation willing to bring under religious scrutiny the material conditions of living. The churches' own willingness to raise these questions about themselves may well become a kind of humanizing, liberative nagging for the wider society.

Habermas describes how current capitalism and the bureaucratic administrations supporting it tend to function within social subsystems freed of all norms except legal ones. These systems spin on, basically without the input of people affected by them and unable to be questioned by those who might ordinarily have some sound hesitations. Once the coordination of action has been transferred from human agents over to what Habermas calls "delinguistified media," such systems become "independent... [of] the value orientations and action dispositions of [ordinary] persons."[31] What ordinary people think and do does not matter. Habermas adds to this analysis an uncharacteristically pithy but chilling contention: "The more complex social systems become, the more provincial lifeworlds become."[32] The result is that many people's humanizing energies are squandered, say, on concern for a celebrity accused of a heinous crime, while massive transfers of armaments, wide-area starvation, or even genocide are overlooked as beyond attention and comment. The problem of diminished reflection among religious groups is, then, not so much that the group soul of religious people is at stake — though indeed it is — but that as a result the *religiously* humanizing vision of the world is missing from the realm of the lifeworld, as are the possibilities of action harbored within that vision. Society is cheated of religious wisdom and the sort of action it funds.

If "the meaning of a tradition is appropriated only in the practical ability to apply it,"[33] gathering together around altars and chanting ritual refrains about the place of the Spirit of Jesus in our lives is a necessary but no longer sufficient condition of discipleship. As a single practice, such activity tends to allow scoundrels and oppressors to leap ahead with their programs unopposed but tends also to mask our own collusion in these programs. We have said holy words; therefore, we are good. To be true to its sacred texts, a local church will reflect critically on the material conditions of living as a normal but essential aspect of its ecclesial life. As noted earlier, such normality is capable of being suppressed,[34] especially in a time when multiple visual narratives about the meaning of existence can be electronically beamed into one's home daily. Stitched into these visual narratives is a complex web of explicit and implicit messages, constructed with a common purpose: to produce in people a desire for purchasable items. In addition the implications for gospel-centered communities of political and economic decisions affecting the fate of millions of persons cannot be gotten by switching to electronic news sources. These decisions need to be submitted to judgment tied both to norms and to accurate, in-depth information.

Conclusion

The Spirit of Jesus becomes accessible through those who gather in his name, struggling to make actual Jesus' reimagination of what it means to be a human being. We have nowhere to turn but to the local ecclesial assemblies and their possibilities for revealing the Christ in our day. These possibilities can probably be realized only by means of a series of communal interpretive strategies, at the core of which is the following perpetual question: What does gospel fidelity mean in our present circumstances? This question is the key one that seems to be missing in so many local churches today. Other important questions may also be missing, but it is the reconstructive task of the local community to search out these questions by whatever alive and honest process it can find. The things that have entered practice without going through discourse must by means of discourse be redirected through the gate of intention — or discarded.

Those who offer guidelines for this process, and some fine guidelines are available,[35] basically point us back to our sacred writings and ask what is of greatest moment there for our current situation.[36] Francis Schüssler Fiorenza suggests three related stances needed in any reconstructive process: standing in solidarity with suffering, becoming a community of discourse, and choosing integrity as a guiding principle.[37] Bonding with those who suffer fosters critique of social structures and our own place in them. Solidarity with human anguish also tends to challenge justifications for the status quo, while sparking back-and-forth conversation toward insight and healing action. Fiorenza's third communal posture, integrity, is a mobile virtue, not a conceptual insight into some pregiven essence of gospel living. By means of integrity, a community becomes accountable for its attention to suffering, for its willingness to consider alternative perspectives and alternative procedures, and, in the end, for the way it actually lives its life. Of these three postures, the one most stubbornly disallowed by the procedures in place in most local churches, including the procedures for worship, is the community of discourse. Only insofar as religious persons come to be full agents in creating a set of coherent, communally embraced practices do they have religious knowledge, religious belief, or make credible religious truth claims. Shared practices are the grounds for shared beliefs.[38]

As I have insisted so often in this book, the cogency among our Christian symbols, doctrines, and practices is not automatically self-maintaining — any more than the vitality of our own limbs is. Applying sweet-smelling lotions will not maintain the elasticity of our limbs; only constant, wise, and vigorous use will keep them vital. The same is true of the symbols, doctrines, and practices of our Christian assemblies. A community's meanings can perdure only if its members work actively out of these meanings, exercising them skillfully so as to get at what they mean for present circumstances. Practice is what enlivens religious meanings, vivifying them in the encounter with current challenges. This encounter demands enlivening conversation about what the assembly's texts mean in the here and now.

Such speech cannot be one-way, from elites who know the right interpretation of the tradition for this current circumstance to the congregation who passively ingest these insights. Such one-way communication does not maintain the community's faith, if only because the dilemmas of current circumstances are not the work of elites but of the entire congregation as an interpretive community seeking faith's implications for these particular circumstances. Enlivened by the struggle for insight, the action of the Christian congregation as a corporate entity enriches the public life of society, where such action rooted in discourse is so badly needed.

The possibilities of local churches committed to the kind of reflection on the material conditions of living at simultaneously local and global levels are not theoretical, but actual. In Latin America, Asia, Africa, and North America can be found communities crying out against suffering and the social structures that cause it. These communities have committed themselves to finding new ways of being the church and of living a gospel practice of solidarity with those who suffer. They reimagine for us the possibilities of the local practice of justice and of reflecting on that practice. Within such communities are "organic intellectuals" or theologians, helping people articulate their gospel response and maintain its connection to wider, global questions. Such leaders are not elites speaking their wisdom to the helpless and inept. Though some of these leaders may have formal theological training, their deeper formation has been in the struggles of the people with whom they speak.[39] They are organic because they have planted themselves within the people. Such local churches show that active communities of interpretation exist not just in someone's fantasy but are actual and functioning. They are actualities making possible the reimagination of the local church and its practice so that the teachings embodied in practice are coherent with and verify the teachings embodied in statements.

Questions for Discussion and Reflection

1. The author warns of dangers in raising the issue of life structure, with the main one being a move to moralizing and cut-and-dried formulas. Can you (a) make more explicit and specific these dangers and (b) specify the conditions under which they could be avoided?

2. What significance might the VALS research have for a pastoral staff of a particular church?

3. What practical value does the notion of habitus have for pastoral ministers in a particular church? Would the ministers and the church be better off to leave the matter untouched? If one were to raise it so it might get a hearing, how might it be done? Is the analogy of the tightrope walker a far-fetched one for the religious habitus? Can you think of other, better analogies?

4. Bourdieu says that many things enter practice without going through discourse. What might be some specific examples to be found in practice in a local church?

5. This chapter makes central claims about the role of judgment in living a gospel life. How possible is it today for ordinary people to adopt the gospel as the basis of day-to-day judgments? Under what conditions might it be possible? What would pastoral agents have to do to help realize those conditions? If it is true that skill in applying gospel norms is a practical art developed gradually over time, how does any of us begin to develop the skills of this art?

6. If life structure develops *primarily* (but not exclusively) out of life decisions, what decisions in your own life have determined your present life structure? Are there decisions, once taken, that can be redecided? Where a decision's outcome cannot be redecided (for example, once children are born, they cannot be redecided), are there aspects of the initial decision that can be, must be, redecided?

7. How might the notion of life structure function in a ministry to young adults?

8. Do you find the issue of financial investments as important as the author claims? Why? How often does such an issue arise in church circles?

9. "The community's practice produces either a radical religious intervention in the world or a domesticated one" (see above p. 118). An undergraduate student once told her teacher this was the kind of statement religious fanatics make. Is there some truth in that student's view?

Analysis of Practices as a Discipline of Resistance

In the history of Christian asceticism a time-honored procedure for examining one's behavior has been by means of questions about patterns of practice. The procedure was called the "examination of conscience" but was, in fact, an examination of behavior. The practice had dangers: focusing approvingly on certain practices as fidelity to the gospel and ignoring wider aspects of behavior or even the attitudes behind behavior. There was also the danger of becoming legalistic. However, followed wisely, the examination of actions helped people be more self-aware and mindful of their behavior.

The following questions are cast in the examination-of-conscience genre as examples of questions that disclose behavior. I offer them hesitantly. If these questions are not helpful, readers may want to devise some that are.

1. When in the course of a day do you say no to a craving?

   • the telephone?

   • the TV?

   • printed advertising?

   • food?

   • work?

   • _____ (something you suspect you should occasionally or always say no to)?

2. When, to have times of silence, do you say no to talk or media?

3. When do you take time to read for reflection or for information, not for entertainment? When do you take time to read for pleasure or nourishment of the imagination? When do you read for religious enrichment?

4. What activity or activities do you need to find time or make time for?

5. How often do you pray and in what ways?

CHAPTER SIX

SPIRIT RESONANCE

The Achievement of Practice

How do we discern the "spirits" good and/or ill at the heart of a particular congregation? To address this question, once more the focus is practice, this time examining Spirit resonance, a view of practice that sheds light on catechesis and discipleship, and some characteristics of transforming, Spirit-filled congregations.

Resonating with the Spirit of Jesus

The Spirit of Jesus is the one who resonates in our midst or who is meant to resonate there. I use the term "resonance," not as an abstraction, but as a "concretion," as a characteristic more subtle than the attentiveness of lovers to one another but still discernible. With "resonance," I am using an auditory metaphor to suggest aliveness or deadness in congregations. The character of resonance is found not just in sound but in a certain quality of sound to which hearers respond. Its quality is one of echoing or reverberation recognizable even in its variances of more and less. There is, for example, a variance between the resonance of a drumbeat and of a fine trained voice, but both have resonance when compared with the sharp, nonresonating sound of a glass shattering on a stone floor. Even if the shattering took place in an acoustically superb church, the echoes might seem resonant in an unpleasant sense as clatter. If one insisted that the shattering was resonant in that church, then I would call it a "tinny" resonance. Lacking deeper resonance, sound is still sound but may take on a character of acoustical annoyance.

Those in a Spirit-resonant community are meant to develop a perceptive system attuned to the gospel the way a parent of an infant can be so psychically tuned to her person that he wakes at night to her slightest cry and immediately attends her needs. When the Spirit of

Jesus resonates in our congregations, it becomes discernible in their gospel practice because resonance involves not just perception but action. Absent the Spirit of Jesus, ecclesial life, though still marked by religious language, is also marked by a basic insensitivity to the demands of the gospel in everyday situations. A specific assembly's life can lack gospel depth or resonance. On the other hand, the Spirit-resonant community tends toward judgments true to the mind of Jesus and action based on judgment. These judgments-become-action are a convincing sign of a gospel-centered pattern of perception. To repeat, the resonance or its lack is discernible in the nuances of a church's group responsiveness.

In a famous essay, Bernard Lonergan describes how in church groups unwise decisions and practices generate further unwise practices, ending in what he calls a "cumulative surd," a serious communal deafness.[1] On the other hand, an intelligent facing of problems tied to a courageous search for solutions can lead to patterns of progress and improvement: a kind of communal responsiveness. Since the English word "absurd" has its roots in Greek and Latin words for deafness, the "absurd" came to name what results from an inability to communicate because of deafness. In a similar vein, I noted in the introduction how married couples can be so emotionally deaf to each other that total strangers are able to "hear" their emotional needs better than their own partner. When that happens, their potentially loving relationship has become actually and discernibly absurd. They have become emotionally deaf to each other.

The attunedness or deafness of communities, like their aliveness or deadness, is powerfully underscored in the recent work of Jerome Bruner, the cultural psychologist. Bruner notes the "grave error" in locating intelligence in a single head,[2] saying it would be much more accurate to see intelligence as distributed, found also in an environment of tools: books, journals, reference tomes, notes based on reading, computers, electronic communications, and so on. It is found in habits of organization, of reflection and study, of relaxation. Even more it is distributed among one's colleagues, friends, and a wide circle of discourse partners, as well as in the habit of actually conversing with them. Research has shown that a person's chances of winning a Nobel prize in science are sharply increased by one's having worked in a laboratory in which an earlier prizewinner had worked. Apparently, the habits of work, the kind of encouragement offered, the atmosphere of creative research established, the allocation of research money — all offer a zone fostering the sort of creativity but also the specific procedures needed for world-class scientific inquiry.

Of course, the notion of distributed intelligence implies a possible dark side: the possibility of distributed obtuseness or deafness. There can be conditions that lend themselves, not to elegant inquiry, but to sloppy science, and these conditions can spill over from particular persons of sloppy habits to a community of persons working in conditions that become, if not hostile to science itself, then at least hostile to a certain level of astute scientific inquiry. Each side of this equation of distributed intelligence has obvious implications for churches. Living in a community whose praxis is embodied in acts of healing carried out in its social and civic environment fosters one sort of "distributive discipleship," while living in one whose praxis is reduced to a weekly ritual of self-affirmation cut off from acts of civic healing produces a quite different sense of discipleship. I have met young people who seem to name their life in church as limited to the practice of doctrinal expertise, an expertise with little interest to them. Any deeper skills of discipleship have been denied them at least implicitly. Such young people joyfully waltz away from ecclesial affiliation altogether, unaware of what an ecclesia is meant to be. They had languished by the Pool of Bethesda, where, inches from transformation, no one assisted them into the healing waters.

In persons and communities, paying attention to religious resonance (understood as "aliveness") is an ancient skill, found throughout the Jewish Scriptures, most clearly perhaps in the prophetic writings. One could argue that Jesus used a similar norm for many of his own judgments about individuals and events. In the case of the widow with the tiny contribution or the man of wealth hesitant to put his goods aside, Jesus discerned depth, in the one case actual, in the other, potential. Ignatius Loyola's Spiritual Exercises are actually procedures for discernment of positive or negative spiritual energies.[3] Discernment in Loyola's usage is a work of determining at the depth of a person's life (i.e., in its assumptions, perceptions, judgments, and decisions) the vital resonance of Jesus' Spirit or the clattery sounds of spiritual illness.

When the monsignors, bishops, archbishops, cardinals, majors, captains, colonels, and various levels of generals gathered in the Roman Catholic cathedral in Buenos Aires during the years young protesters were murdered, holy words, holy gestures, and an ancient ritual were enacted, but there was no resonance of the Spirit of Jesus. An important theological controversy could erupt over the question of whether there was a Eucharist at all. One could say the event was an active catechesis of death, a powerful anticatechesis that found the murder of the innocent ones to be unconnected to the Good News of the crucified one. The Buenos Aires catechesis of absurdity proclaimed this: the church celebrates, not the crucified one who protested all injustice, but dominative power. Unfortunately, when a community is deaf to the gospel, their communal life may lumber along but at the heart of it is a profound inattentiveness to the gospel, that is, Lonergan's "cumulative surd." For a community to be Christian, somewhere in it will be found observable gospel characteristics, such as sensitivity to Jesus' announcement of good news for the poor. These characteristics become discernible in the community's practice.

Ways of Thinking about Practice

The most common way of thinking about ecclesial practice is to take it for granted and refuse to give it a second, more careful glance. We tell ourselves we understand it, we know what it is about, and it is no problem. The practice thus comes under no scrutiny, critical or otherwise. It just is. Priest friends tell me that the most usual way local church practice gets the bishop's attention is when it does not produce the income the bishop has decided should be donated to diocesan funds. In such a case, there is sure to be close episcopal scrutiny but of fiscal matters only, with the actual gospel practice overlooked or taken for granted.

This ignoring of practice contrasts with the intense scrutiny given practice by the market researchers described in chapter 5 (see above pp. 101ff.). Since James Atlas wrote his account of VALS research, the study of shopping habits has progressed rapidly. The emerging specialty of "retail anthropology" sets up videos camera both outside and inside stores as a way of studying the behavior of shoppers as they approach a store, enter it, and make their way into its recesses. Trained observers are positioned in the store with their clipboards at the ready to jot down observations that might be missed by the cameras. From these studies, retail anthropology can tell retailers that on average a U.S. shopper's visit to a shopping mall in 1995 was sixty-six minutes, the shortest ever recorded. Other disturbing data on shopper habits in a particular store of a clothing chain found that "purchasers...spent an average of eleven minutes and twenty-two seconds in the store, nonpurchasers two minutes and thirty-six seconds" even though they "examined an average of 3.42 items."[4] Readers might be wondering if I am suggesting the local church is the "store" where worshipers "buy" the religious product. Far from it. Instead, in my puzzlement over why ecclesial practice receives so little critical attention, I am struck at how in an entirely different kind of practice, retail selling, interest in profits drives minutely planned and focused attention to patterns of behavior in shopping. Interest in gospel fidelity might properly direct the attention of Christians to the particulars of faith-filled behavior. As already stated, I am not looking for moralizing about formulaic behavioral correctives. My concern is for more studied, critical attention to what we are about as persons who profess to be followers of Jesus of Nazareth.

In this book thus far I have used the word "practice" in two different ways. The first was to name a range of activities used by local churches as a way of being a church, in other words, the things we do. In fact, this whole book is a reflection on practice in the sense of what we do regularly and ordinarily. Most of these activities are quasi-intentional in the sense they often become so routinized and are done with such inattention that they should be reexamined, though they are not. Indeed, these practices should be brought through the gate of religious intention to insure they do what we want or intend them to do, notwithstanding the recognition that practices always do more or other than we intend. The second meaning comes from Pierre Bourdieu, who uses the word "practice" to mean the activities in which we engage, but his focus is on those activities that tend to be at the margins of our awareness. This is an aspect of practice not often considered. Since this side of practice shapes us, especially our attitudes or spirits, all thoughtful people might profitably consider it, but religious people *must* do so.

A third meaning, which I have consciously avoided in this book, is practice as "praxis," that is, practice as used in Marxist analysis to name a self-creating and world-creating activity tied to theoretical considerations, as distinct from the kind of action motivated by routine and habit. Though I have not explored praxis here, this book itself is an exercise in just this sense of practice. Marxist praxis names human activity flowing from active social awareness and a consciousness of theory: intentionality in spades or what Max Weber and others call "instrumental rationality." Bourdieu's usage is so much the reverse of this Marxist praxis that he claims to never use the term "praxis."[5]

In the following section I am going to use "practice" with yet another meaning, one from philosophy that I find to have value for thinking about discipleship and about catechesis as a ministry to practice. Philosopher Alisdair MacIntyre describes this meaning as follows:

By a "practice" I...mean any coherent and complex form of
socially established cooperative human activity through which
goods internal to that form of activity are realized in the course
of trying to achieve those standards of excellence which are appropriate to, and partially definitive of, that form of activity,
with the result that human powers to achieve excellence and
human conceptions of the ends and goods involved are system-
atically extended. Tic-tac-toe is not an example of a practice in
this sense nor is throwing a football with skill; but the game of
football is and so is chess.... Planting turnips is not a practice;
farming is....[6]

In my own words, practice in this sense is a complex form of human
activity that has evolved by means of common effort aimed at not
only doing well the activity the practice represents but improving it
consistently and strenuously by efforts to achieve and even go beyond
the standards of good practice, thus enlarging and refining these standards. Gradually, the practice itself improves and changes because the
standards of practice become better. A case in point might be athletic
standards, especially in track-and-field events. Not everything involving
skill is a practice. A practice becomes a practice in MacIntyre's sense
only when a number of persons recognize the skill it involves, study
the particular behaviors of that skill, try to improve on it — and in the
end see that it is worth considerable human effort. Tic-tac-toe does not
qualify as this kind of practice; neither does blowing big bubbles with
bubblegum.

A practice then is a set of activities defined by its search for excellence. This kind of practice is founded in a body of persons, most
of whom may never meet and not all of whom even live at the same
moment in history, but all of whom have embraced the standards of
the practice. What these people have in common is that they have
submitted themselves to the evolving excellence of the practice at the
same time they have submitted the practice to their own fruitful creativity. Willingly, eagerly, patiently, they have submitted themselves to
the discipline of the practice. Together they have accepted challeng-
ing standards tending to be beyond them. No one measures up to such
standards easily but only gradually, over time, by taking seriously the
integrity demanded by the practice itself. In other words, the discipline required is not an obstacle since it both fosters the flourishing
of enablement and celebrates achievement.

In a gymnastics session, a group of children ages eleven to thirteen are all intent on the efforts of the one on the parallel bars. Their rapt attention and her intense sweating effort create a tangible stillness in the room. Gasps accompany her unsuccessful moves, but at one brilliantly executed turn, the group erupts in excited cheers of affirmation. She dismounts, smiles, and bows to her fellow fledglings, acknowledging their appreciation of her efforts. This is the flourishing of enablement and the celebration of achievement. In the very process of enhancing its practitioners, a practice itself is enhanced. It evolves as it accrues classic creative forms and becomes more complex. Its history expands.

If I am lost and hungry in the woods, equipped with a simple drop fishing line to which is attached a sinker and a hook, I may be able almost by chance to catch a trout for food. It would be difficult, but I might succeed, though my success would not mean I have entered the practice of fly-fishing. However, if after my rescue I wish to become competent at fly-fishing, I will need more than the proper equipment. The equipment allows me to engage in the activity of fly-fishing; the *practice* of fly-fishing is something else. For that I also need to acquaint myself with the best practitioners of the skill and maybe also with written accounts of this practice that date back hundreds of years. If I become aware of a wide international community of persons who work at this practice, I may seek a chance to meet and question some of them about how they approach one or another problem of flexible-rod fishing.

A more ordinary example of a practice might be the parenting of children. Someone might object there is no discipline to this practice, since anyone who knows how to be loving and judicious in dealing with a child can parent. True, but those who have parented at a high level of awareness and skill have provided written accounts of their own trials and errors and of how they came to wisdom on various aspects of parenting. The person who is naturally most loving and judicious towards children might be just the sort of person who wants to know more about the practice of parenting — and to engage the wisdom of a centuries-old community of persons who have distilled for each other the best of the wisdom of parenting.

Examples of practices, as fly-fishing and family development (parenting) might suggest, are endless and varied, even when listed alphabetically: falconry, farming, fencing, filming, fishing, flower gardening, footballing, framing. Each of these practices has generated a past and present literature reflecting on its standards of excellence. Today most practices have their own periodical literature. Despite these evidences of robustness, a practice is brittle. Not all practices endure. A practice can lose its ability to spark the energies of potential practitioners. When this happens, a practice eventually dies out as practitioners abandon their efforts to expand and develop its standards.

Catechesis and Practice

Catechesis has discrete activities for fostering an ever-maturing living faith. Some of these have to do with preparing persons for "next steps" in the development of their faith. Other activities encourage reflection on communal dilemmas facing discipleship at a particular time and in a particular locale. The purpose of catechesis is the flourishing of discipleship, and the mode of catechesis is the celebration of discipleship. Is catechesis, then, a practice? I think not because catechesis is not a discrete set of activities. It is part of a larger activity, the practice of discipleship, the following of the way outlined by Jesus of Nazareth and his followers. In fact, as a discrete practice, an activity unto itself, catechesis becomes distorted. While catechesis has standards of excellence, those standards measure not catechesis but the excellence of discipleship.

Discipleship is a practice with a two-millennia history and abundant literature attesting to centuries of effort toward this practice. Like any practice, discipleship is found only partially in written texts about it but most fully in the flourishing practice of present-day practitioners, growing in proficiency in the crafts of discipling. The community of this practice celebrates all levels of this proficiency, with special recognition given the achievements of virtuoso practitioners, individual and communal, present and past. These have often been called saints or saintly. Representing a particularly skillful level of practice, these virtuosos exhibit an enhanced standard.

Catechesis is not primarily activity toward mastering the theoretical concepts involved in its own catechetical activities; it is primarily about the practice of discipleship. The work of catechesis is reminding the community of the standards of excellence they have adopted and the kind of responsiveness those standards demand from those who are, or are trying to become, practitioners. Catechesis provides reminders about conditions under which practice is diminished or enhanced or cautious. The eye of catechesis is on the community's practice, not its catechetical practice, but on the discipling practice to which catechesis points. Catechesis fosters the efforts of the community to maintain its standard of discipling practice. Catechesis is the coaching of a practice.

In recent centuries, catechesis has tended to lose its way, becoming a practice unto itself instead of pointing to the practice of discipleship. It has become an activity about ideas, giving the impression that correct understanding represents adequate practice, whereas in fact that understanding directs and redirects the actual practice. Consequently, communities engaged in "churchly practices" have been able to remove themselves from preoccupation with discipleship itself.

The Economy of a Practice

If we look at a practice from the inside, that is, from the perspective of someone engaging in its activities, then we see that the economy of a practice is not a stingy one based on scarcity. Instead, its economy is based on ampleness and inclusivity. The inner enrichment a practice offers is accessible to all its practitioners. It is not like a pot of soup, which might not yield enough for all if some take too much. The excellences of a practice are available to anyone who cares to delight in them. Practice is a hen laying endless golden eggs. My developing my talents in a practice diminishes no other person's flourishing efforts. Indeed, just the opposite is true. My flourishing practice models for others features they may wish to incorporate into theirs; my discipline in the practice may encourage similar discipline in another. In this sense, practice is a sacred cup that becomes more full as it is passed and savored.

Regarding practice, fledgling efforts, like those of the young gymnasts in their glimmerings of virtuosity, enrich all. All levels of accomplishment — but also the sense of aliveness and accomplishment they demonstrate — are part of the wider practice. At all levels, achievements can be admired, emulated, and celebrated.[7] A child of five does a self-portrait in watercolors. He does it quickly, in a matter of minutes. Yet in the contours given his own face, accurate even in their exaggeration, and in the various symbols he has included to express his self, an accomplished artist recognizes an astonishing capacity of self-awareness and self-expression with color and line. To be sure, the portrait is that done by a five-year-old, not by a twenty-five-year-old. Still its elements of originality and spirit fit it into the practice of portraiture and call for celebration, in the form, say, of framing and hanging it.

If catechesis is viewed as an activity of the knowing well-informed toward the unknowing uninformed, then its economy is one of scarcity healed by handouts. This exchange represents the heart of a market economy: I have the goods you need. But if we see catechesis as a communal practice encouraging in all skill in living "the Jesus way," then the five-year-old can enter that practice with integrity and with a grace appropriate to one his age. There are endless routes to integrity in a practice, and they can all be true practice. The possibilities are ample not scarce. The seven-year-old soccer player does not possess the proficiency of the thirty-year-old Brazilian star, but she is truly playing soccer, not baseball. How does one encourage her interest in the practice of soccer? What is the proper ratio of instruction, practice, and competition? One might ask how many classroom instructions about soccer it will take to diminish decisively her interest or even capacity for soccer. On the other hand, she cannot be pushed into a love for soccer; she comes to it the way the child above picks up a brush and uses paint as a way of getting at something real.

If a child enters the communal activity of catechesis by intentionally placing herself within the circle of learning to know and practice discipleship — in other words, if she has not been shoved unwillingly into that circle — then her practice simultaneously enriches and is enriched by the surrounding practice of all. In fact, the prayer of the five-year-old might spark admiration or even awe in the forty-five-year-old. At all levels of achievement, authentic practice can be celebrated. At all age levels, further achievement is possible; the goods of practice are for life itself, not just for its early stages.

Intrinsic and Extrinsic Goods of a Practice

Connected to every practice are internal and external goods or benefits, but the external are secondary. The external goods of fishing can be obtained by means other than actually fishing. Fish can be gotten for dinner without the eaters engaging in fishing, for money will allow one to purchase for a tasty dinner fish others have caught. For that matter, money enables one to buy an attention-getting stuffed trophy of a fish someone else netted. Awards, another external good, may stand for accomplishment in a practice long ago abandoned. Whatever the value of the external goods — those benefits that come when one has stepped away from actual practice — the goods internal to the activity itself are prior and must be prized for the practice to be engaged. Among these intrinsic goods of a practice are human qualities refined by its discipline: patience, honesty, and judgment regarding one's own practice; generosity, cooperation, and appreciation regarding the practice of others. These goods can spill over into the life of one devoted to practice.[8]

One cannot enter a practice without prizing the good-of-it intrinsic to the activity itself. Among these internal rewards must also be counted objective achievements that flow from the practice: a productive farm, a well-crafted frame, a victory or championship at football, or a film that can be screened. On the other hand, the external goods may or may not come to practitioners: wealth, status, reputation. These goods eluded the British artist-poet William Blake in his lifetime.[9] Overfocus on the external rewards of a practice may seriously erode that practice by losing touch with its inner integrity. I tell my students that while I am paid (external rewards) to teach, I would certainly be willing to pay to be able teach (because of its internal rewards). Of course, lacking *any* external rewards or goods, the practitioner may be tempted to give up the practice altogether. Some sort of harmony between the two seems called for.

Catechetical Connections

The kinds of external goods usually found in a practice are not found in the practice of discipleship. Actually the integrity of the practice of discipleship may call for disdaining external rewards such as money or fame or power. The complexity of this can be seen in the matter of power. Discipleship may call one to reject money as a goal in life, but power and fame are more subtle, open to being prized even when explicitly rejected. "Mammon" was the word used early in the Christian tradition to connote how one might deny a good to oneself only to take pride in the "possession" of the self-denial. In embracing poverty, one could become rich in one's sense of having bettered others by pursuing a more admirable poverty.[10]

The internal goods of discipleship basically come from one's relationship with God and from the struggle to fashion a human way of being in keeping with God's designs, as disclosed by Jesus. The second greatest of these internal goods is objective or tangible: the loveliness of a life exhibiting fidelity to the example of Jesus and his tradition. Any ritual act, a beautiful hymn for example, finds its meaning and even fruition in such a life. The greatest objective good of discipleship is the loveliness of a community exhibiting the risks of practiced discipleship. Joseph Dunne points out that the original sense of practice, especially as found in Aristotle, is "the practice of living, more especially living as a member of a community...and as a citizen of the polity. Here 'good' takes on its capacities of deliberation and judgment and for the exercise of moral and civic virtues."[11]

The "way of being" as the compelling internal good of discipleship is also discernible to others. This fact is powerfully brought forward in the memoirs of a nineteenth-century French bishop, Felix Dupanloup. He recounts the impression the goodness of his catechists made on him as a young child, attending catechetical sessions in the Church of Saint Sulpice in Paris. Even accounting for the nostalgic glow and the almost domesticating emphasis of such a memory from the past, his account is powerful:

> [T]he first instinct of a child, when the child has the happiness of meeting with noble and benevolent souls...is a deep-seated and excellent instinct; it is the true respect for oneself and for them; it is the good and right desire to make oneself loved by those one admires; but in order to do this, the child must feel that she is in a place where she can hope to be esteemed and loved...; that one is in a place where souls are regarded closely and lovingly; where good behavior, virtue, and docility are held in honor; where they are taught, where they are learnt, *where they are practiced; where those are loved and esteemed who are not yet good* [emphasis added] but who wish to become so, who have a good will for it and have already made some happy beginnings. In short a child must feel that catechesis is a school of wisdom and virtue, presided over by kindness, affection, devotion, the love of God and the love of souls; where, under the auspices of a religious and fatherly discipline, are found the support of good examples, the sweetness of friendship, the inspiration of gratitude and the excitement and generosity of Christian emulation....
>
> Thenceforth I began to love my catechists; their gravity, their gentleness, their kindness, attracted me to them. I had a great desire to win their favor and their regard....I did not say this to myself in so many words, but I felt it.[12]

Later Dupanloup sums up this memory: "[N]owhere else in the world did our childhood receive such consideration."[13]

Practice and Perception

Surely it must be obvious that "practice" as described by MacIntyre and Dunne does not come naturally or even easily. Like the child on the parallel bars, sweating and uncertain in her efforts to excel, the faithful local congregation will come to this kind of discipling practice only gradually — endlessly gradually. Indeed, I doubt there can be an effective renewal of the local church without an active, ongoing, and endless communal discussion of the dilemmas of fidelity to God's call today.

Though procedures are needed for such a discussion to be operative, the chief problem affecting the local churches today is not fundamentally a procedural problem. The chief problem is that of perception, of the mindset that we bring to our everyday lives. Another way of putting it: the spirit we embody in our lives may not be the Spirit of Christ Jesus. A risky example may show what I have in mind here. When a person meets another whose wholesome human goodness is thoroughly enchanting, one may want to be companioned by this goodness for a lifetime. When that happens, the human faculty most deeply engaged is the imagination. The first person's imagination becomes in a sense taken over and inhabited by the beloved. In a sense, in the body of the lover dwell not one person but two. At least that's how it feels to many. The lover has been taken over by an imagination of the beloved, which will gradually be verified, adjusted, and nuanced *continually* throughout the duration of the relationship. Still, the shift in the imagination occasioned by the beloved alters everything: one's sense of the present, one's sense of oneself, and dramatically, one's hopes for the future. One's perception has been taken over by the mind-altering event of enchantment. One begins to see the world differently.

In the New Testament Epistles, I find many passages brimming with the shift of perception analogous to erotic enchantment. In Colossians, Paul reminds his readers of "the mystery of Christ in you, your hope of glory" (1:27) and, later, of his hope they will "be closely united in love, enriched with full assurance by . . . knowledge of the mystery of God — namely Christ" (2:2). Still further on, he clearly focuses on loving perception: "Let the word of Christ, rich as it is, dwell in you" (3:16). This metaphor of "inhabitation" by Christ runs through all these letters. Notice the "innerness" of these words from Ephesians: "I pray that the God of our Lord Jesus Christ, the God of glory, may give you a spirit of wisdom and revelation as you come to know him, so that, with your eyes enlightened, you may know what is the hope to which you have been called . . . , and what is the immeasurable greatness of God's power for us who believe, according to the working of God's great power" (1:17–19, Oxford Inclusive Version).

It is no wonder the word chosen to name the process by which these convictions inhabit a person is "conversion," that is "shift" or "change," because of their import for the way one will act. Conversion affects one's spirit, one's spirituality, the way one encounters the world, one's way of perceiving and interpreting events. As the writer of Ephesians later says, "You must put on that new person created in God's image" (4:24). I find the same metaphoric underpinning in the Gospel parables of the seed sown into the earth in which it becomes fruitful, which itself is an echo of Isaiah 55:10–11, where the prophet reminds Israel that God's word is like seed become fruitful and then eaten as bread. Praying the ancient liturgical prayer The Confiteor symbolizes this need for repentance as a condition of worship. The Confiteor is like the act of taking off one's shoes and walking unshod onto the prayer rug.

Overlooking the complications of interiorizing a gospel perspective and perception today would be folly. The same would be true of overlooking the complications of erotic enchantment. The highly pleasurable events of enchantment must give way to a commitment to the beloved that will prove true even in moments of disenchantment, or when there is need to put aside personal ego to meet the needs of the beloved. Indeed, the one initially enchanted may at some point wonder how a relationship so effortless in its initial stages has moved to such struggle. Shifts in perception leading to new ways of living are rarely automatic or simple. To paraphrase Berger and Luckmann, conversion is no big deal; the big deal is the maintenance of conversion.

The New Testament exhortations and reminders cited above were written to communities *seeking* to embody a radically shifted perceptive system, "eyes enlightened" as Paul puts it. Those messages from the apostolic virtuosos verified what the communities were trying to live. They named it. However, even as these letters were written and as they were read, there was in the background a culture hostile to them, able to scoff at a "weird" imagination of life. Yet the communities to whom they were addressed did not find these exhortations weird because in the foreground as they were being heard, that is, in the very context of their being announced, was a community open to those messages. The foreground community was maintaining the conversion through its contact with other communities of "alternative practice."

My hunch is that the messages we ourselves have access to daily "in living color" — their explicit foreground messages laced with implicit background convictions — can make people profoundly deaf to the wisdom of the Christic mindset and "lifeset." The Spirit resonance I have tried to suggest above is a way of naming the shift in perception necessary for gospel living. As the writer of Philippians puts it, "Let the same mind be in you that was in Christ Jesus" (2:5). What are some characteristics of communities who live out that mind of Christ Jesus? This is the next and concluding matter of this book.

Characteristics of a Local Church of Vital Practice

As I have been composing this study, I often found myself asking what might be some characteristics of a local church that was embodying the practice of discipleship. I hesitated to construct examples for fear they would close off the ongoing creative struggle to meet the needs of a particular place and time. Examples, especially theoretical ones, may defeat a whole line of thought by inviting a reader to say, "Aha, so *that's* what this is all about," whereas what this is really about is keeping open questions creatively open and constantly discovering discipleship a step at a time.

I offer the following brief descriptions of some "model" characteristics of local churches in hopes that readers will question them, critique them, reconceive them, and, best of all, develop a process by which a local church can come to its own statement of the characteristics it seeks to embody. Should a congregation attempt to do so, they might try to ground any statement of characteristics in the New Testament.

Attitudinal Characteristics

An appreciation of the gifts of discipleship in the community; a sense of the distinctive embodiments of the gospel by individuals and the community in distinctive situations; an appreciation and affirmation of the gospel practice of other local churches of any denomination. This appreciation involves the ability to name and celebrate gospel-related gifts. The procedures of naming and celebrating would be predominantly informal but endemic (i.e., "in and among the people").

The Roman Catholic diocesan newspapers I have seen are quick to name and celebrate the achievements of diocesan laypersons who have risen to the corporate hierarchy, who have contributed large sums to the church, who have achieved sports or other media-related kinds of fame. Rarely do I find celebrated in either individuals or groups more gospel-centered gifts, such as giving wise counsel to the confused, visiting the sick (especially when it is inconvenient for the visitor to do so), comforting the dying, feeding the hungry, spending a year or more in service to those on the social margins, and taking risks in the name of discipleship. Not complaint, my point here is observation of a missing agenda in our deciding what is noteworthy.

In many religious orders I find this "missing agenda" present and active. The religious congregation I know best regularly celebrates the "plenitude" of various members who have died. By "plenitude" I do not mean only the accomplishments of those who have died but rather the connection between their gospel gifts and their struggles. I claim that some of these eulogies are masterpieces of hagiography.

A sense of brotherhood and sisterhood in Christ with one another. This is also a sense of collegiality, specifically the collegiality of discipleship fostering a readiness to hear one another and to share with one another. The community has a sense they share in common the Spirit of Jesus. This sense marks their coming together.

Communion with one another in the Spirit of Jesus allows the community to respect disagreements and tolerate differences, while working gradually toward common understandings.[14] Issues may divide the community but not in the sense they forget their unity in God.

Though sisterhood and brotherhood evoke a family metaphor, our sisterhood and brotherhood cannot be defined by what defines the family: intimacy. The ecclesial sisterhood and brotherhood is real but not necessarily intimate. Perhaps "mystical" is the word that best describes the relationship. The loving relationships these words suggest are agapeic, naming those who might not care to share a beer together but who will work side by side to shelter the homeless.[15]

A sense of the community's distinctiveness, based on an appreciation of its particularity. The community at this time and in this place has worked at understanding its call in these specific circumstances. This sense of particularity leads to celebrations of the community and its specialness. Festivity marks its gatherings.

This sense of distinctiveness coexists in tension with an important lack of self-congratulation and an awareness of the incompleteness of its efforts. The "more still to be done" is tied to a conviction that God's agency is the germinating life source in all situations. The community's awareness of the inadequacy of its efforts is tied to an understanding of the human condition. Where a community is marked by self-congratulation — sometimes found in the churches of the well-off and comfortable — it may be a sign of its deep need for conversion.

Procedural Characteristics

A habit of discernment and interpretation of situations developed as a skill by the whole community. Communally they agree to assemble the information necessary for such interpretation. They develop over time a perceptive system rooted in the Good News.

A set of clear, named gospel priorities embraced by the community in the light of its local situation. These priorities call for short-term and long-term action, as well as a regular reexamination of these priorities in the face of changing situations.

Regular attention to in-depth "Christian formation" (formation of a gospel spirit and practice) among the community's members. This formation, though not always done in an explicitly festive mode, honors the celebrative as a character proper to gatherings in Jesus' name. Formation properly done calls for and receives an extravagant use of the community's attention, time, and energy, equivalent to the lavish use of a precious vial of oil to wash someone's feet.[16] Community members understand, for example, that preparation for marriage is part of lifelong Christian formation, not a one-time preparation for a wedding.[17]

Search for a gospel practice as a concern of all members. Gospel practice is the active concern of the entire community, not just of its leaders. Initially it may have to be a preoccupation of leaders, but to the degree it does not percolate through the community, it remains inert.

Other Characteristics

Attractiveness of the community's life to young people and others seeking an integrating religious practice who present themselves as candidates for membership. The community in turn is attentive to those who enter its circle of faith, welcoming them into the collegiality of disciples and willing to help them, when ready, to discern their gifts. The young at any age find here a place where their distinctive gifts are honored.

A clear welcome to the tentative or marginally committed. These find in the community the psychic space they need and any assistance they desire for "next steps" in discipleship. They are revered, not as potential members, but as the actual beloved ones of God.

Genuine opportunities for those who might take part in programs to join in planning them. Once the programs are in operation, those participating regularly "have a voice" about how they should proceed. Protocols of participation call for continual scrutiny and adjustment.

•

The sketch offered in the last few pages is an attempt to say what a local church struggling to live the gospel might be like, at least in some of its characteristics. But readers will readily recognize that even this sketch is more general than specific. Our imaginations want the help of specifics when dealing with the implications of ideas. Sometimes when we want to express a reality that seems to defy expression, we resort to the concrete images of poetry to spark insight. Life is about the specifics. The specifics of our local church's "moment" and of its social location — and of the personalities in our ecclesia — make up the stuff out of which fidelity to the God of Jesus can come. The challenge is to struggle with the implications of our Good News in the here and now, for us, these people who gather together in Jesus' name at this time and in this place.

To be sure, there are specific examples available to us. In every area of the country there are *some* local assemblies that exhibit the struggling fidelity I have mentioned so often in these pages. If I want to improve as a photographer, I do well to study shimmering examples of excellent photography. I will search out these examples as a way of honoring excellence but also of directing my own practice. Our Eucharistic assemblies might do the same, not in a search for perfection but as a way of stimulating our imaginations regarding the possibilities of a credible local church.[18] Imagination and heart were two qualities of Jesus himself. This book has been about a renewed imagination of the local church for those who have the heart to pursue it.

Notes

Introduction

1. Shoshana Felman, "Psychoanalysis and Education: Teaching Terminable and Interminable," *Yale French Studies* 63 (1982): 21–44.

2. Here I have paraphrased a paragraph from P. N. Medvedev and M. M. Bakhtin, *The Formal Method in Literary Scholarship*, ed. Albert J. Wehrle (Baltimore: Johns Hopkins University Press, 1978), 7.

3. See Daniel Goleman, "Marriage Research Reveals Ingredients of Happiness," in *Perspectives on Marriage: A Reader*, ed. Kieran Scott and Michael Warren (New York: Oxford University Press, 1993), 249–53.

4. I accept the basic position spelled out by Reinhard Hutter in "Ecclesial Ethics, the Church's Vocation, and Paraclesis," *Pro Ecclesia* 2, no. 4 (fall 1993): 433–50. Efforts can be undertaken in the name of fidelity that would never be taken in the name of success. Fidelity puts the call of God at the center of the struggle to be an ecclesia that indeed does signal the presence of the Spirit.

5. Maybe the best models for such a renewal among Roman Catholics are found in religious congregations of men and women, where renewed structures of speaking and of recognizing gifts are being developed by all for all.

6. As I was finishing my revisions on this book, I started reading the works of Emmanuel Lévinas, where I found the core idea of this paragraph already set forth with great clarity. See, for example, Annette Aronowicz's "Translator's Introduction" and Lévinas's own "Introduction to Four Talmudic Readings" in Emmanuel Lévinas, *Nine Talmudic Readings* (Bloomington: University of Indiana Press, 1994), ix–xxxix and 3–11.

7. Margaret R. Miles, *Practicing Christianity: Critical Perspectives for an Embodied Spirituality* (New York: Crossroad, 1988), 2.

Chapter 1: The Worshiping Assembly

1. For an elaboration of "what jumps out at us," see my "Jungmann and the Kerygmatic Theology Controversy," in Michael Warren, *Sourcebook for Modern Catechetics*, vol. 1 (Winona, Minn.: St. Mary's Press, 1983), 193–98.

2. I agree with Reinhard Hutter that prayer is the center of all the church's practices, indeed of its vocation. Reinhard Hutter, "Ecclesial Ethics, the Church's Vocation, and Paraclesis," *Pro Ecclesia* 2, no. 4 (fall 1993): 433–50, esp. 436–38.

3. Not only were no voices raised around that cathedral altar, but the apostolic nuncio, or papal delegate, Pio Laghi recommended that the church and

the armed forces be coresponsible for what was being done, with the church supporting the armed forces "with its prayers" and with "actions in defense and promotion of human rights and the fatherland." An authoritative source claims that of eighty active cardinals, archbishops, and bishops, only four spoke out against the military junta and their violation of human rights. See Carlos Alberto Torres, *The Church, Society, and Hegemony: A Critical Sociology of Religion in Latin America*, trans. Richard A. Young (London and Westport, Conn.: Praeger, 1992), 167–71.

4. Among Roman Catholics, this question has taken the form of the distinction between sacrament as *opus operatum* and as *opus operantis*. The first, literally "the deed done" or "the work worked," is the unambiguous and efficacious word of God present and available in ritual; the second, literally "the work of the one doing the work," involves the subjective dispositions of those who worship. This distinction was a way of countering reformers' claims that the Roman Church saw sacraments as magical rites. This distinction also asserted that God's power worked in the sacraments beyond the holiness, or lack of it, of the chief celebrant.

Rahner implies that few worshipers see sacraments as magical: "*In individual instances of personally unenlightened people* [emphasis added] a concrete Christian can misunderstand the sacraments in a magical way and also does in fact misunderstand them." However, I believe that many Christian people, including leaders, have what might be called a "nuanced misunderstanding" of the power of sacraments that overstates their efficacy. Not so bald as the magical misunderstanding possessed by Rahner's odd, misinformed person, such a misunderstanding tends to be unwilling to situate worship in the total life of the church. See Karl Rahner, *Foundations of Christian Faith* (New York: Seabury Press, 1978), 413–15.

5. Catherine Bell gets at this question in her various ways of naming ritual and the ritual body. See "The Ritual Body and the Dynamics of Ritual Power," *Journal of Ritual Studies* 4, no. 2 (1990): 299–313.

6. It is possible to find clues to this overstated sacramental efficacy in some passages of Vatican Council II's liturgical document, but only if these passages are taken out of their context in a well-nuanced treatise. For example, see the following passage:

> For it is through the liturgy, especially the divine Eucharistic Sacrifice, that the work of our redemption is exercised. The liturgy is thus the outstanding means by which the faithful can express in their lives, and manifest to others, the mystery of Christ and the real nature of the true Church.... Day by day the liturgy builds up those within the Church into the Lord's holy temple, into a spiritual dwelling for God.... At the same time the liturgy marvelously fortifies the faithful in capacity to preach Christ.
>
> ...The liturgy is considered an exercise of the priestly office of Jesus Christ. In the liturgy the sanctification of man is manifested by signs per-

ceptible to the sense, and is effected in a way which is proper to each of these signs; in the liturgy full public worship is performed by the Mystical Body of Jesus Christ, that is, by the Head and His members.

From this it follows that every liturgical celebration, because it is an action of Christ the priest and of His Body the Church, is a sacred action surpassing all others. *No other action of the church can match its claim to efficacy, nor equal the degree of it* [emphasis added].

See *Constitution on the Sacred Liturgy*, in W. M. Abbott and J. Gallagher, eds., *The Documents of Vatican II* (New York: Association Press, 1966), 137–38, 141.

7. Bell, "The Ritual Body," 302.

8. Aloysius Pieris, "Christianity and Buddhism in Core-to-Core Dialogue," *Cross Currents* 37, no. 1 (spring 1987): 57. In the same passage Pieris expresses optimism about Christianity's ability to perdure: "Both Buddhism and Christianity are vibrant with life because each has developed its own religious system — doctrines, rites, and institutions — which make the original experience available to contemporary society."

9. Geoffrey Wainwright, *Doxology: The Praise of God in Worship, Doctrine, and Life* (New York: Oxford University Press, 1980), 2–3.

10. Ibid., 8. Philosopher John Macmurray makes a similarly obvious point from a different but converging angle. He writes that "community is [a] matter of intention and therefore problematical. What is celebrated is not a fact, but an achievement; and the community has to be maintained in the future.... The individual members of a community must... know the significance of the religious ritual in which they participate, for if not, it can have no significance." John Macmurray, *Persons in Relation* (London: Faber and Faber, 1961), 163.

11. See *Constitution on the Sacred Liturgy*, in Abbott and Gallagher, *The Documents of Vatican II*, 143.

12. Ibid., 142. Notice that the previous passage cited calls for the matching of thoughts and words. This passage, which actually comes earlier in the document, suggests a necessary (and prior) correlative: that words must be matched by lived commitments.

13. Both quotations are found in D. Capelle, "L'Introduction du catechumenat a Rome," *Recherches de théologie ancienne et médievale* 5 (1933): 151 nn. 38 and 39. Capelle gives the original references as Hom. V, 6 in Iud. and C. Cels. 3, 59. Regis Duffy first called my attention to this source.

14. Regis Duffy, *On Becoming a Catholic: The Challenge of Christian Initiation* (San Francisco: Harper and Row, 1984), 44.

15. As I understand it, *lex vivendi* was the whole point of the literature on the ascetical life, which goes back to early Christianity, but that assumed almost a literary form in the eighteenth and nineteenth centuries. On this point, see Sandra Schneiders, "Theology and Spirituality: Strangers, Rivals, or Partners?" *Horizons* 13, no. 2 (1986): 253–74.

16. "Life practice" and "life structure" are not synonyms but are connected. Life practice(s), when repeated, come to be embedded in structures of behavior,

i.e., life structure. A person's daily decisions about buying on credit eventually can create a debilitating debt structure that goes beyond any individual purchase, but becomes a central issue, or even obstacle, in one's life. The word "structure" suggests the tendency toward rigidity or immutability that practice produces.

17. Charles Sanders Peirce, "How to Make Our Ideas Clear," *Writings of Charles Sanders Peirce: A Chronological Edition*, vol. 3 (Bloomington: Indiana University Press, 1986), 263–64.

18. Thomas M. Finn, "Ritual Process and the Survival of Early Christianity: A Study of the Apostolic Tradition of Hippolytus," *Journal of Ritual Studies* 3, no. 1 (winter 1989): 73.

19. Jacques Ellul, *The Subversion of Christianity* (Grand Rapids: Eerdmans, 1986), 4.

20. Mark Searle, "Renewing the Liturgy — Again," *Commonweal*, 18 November 1988, 620.

21. Most of the Williams corpus deals with this question. For a brief statement, see "Means of Communication as Means of Production," in *Problems in Materialism and Culture* (London: Verso Editions, 1980), 50–63.

22. John Kavanaugh, "The World of Wealth and the Gods of Wealth," in *Option for the Poor: Challenge to the Rich Countries*, ed. L. Boff and V. Elizondo, Concilium 187 (Edinburgh: T. and T. Clark, 1986): 17.

23. See Pierre Bourdieu, *Distinction: A Social Critique of the Judgement of Taste* (Cambridge: Harvard University Press, 1984), 101. Here I paraphrase the sense of his argument, found in so many of his writings. The very same claim is made in Samuel Bowles and Herbert Gintis, "The Economy Produces the People: Introduction to Post-Liberal Democracy," in *Religion and Economic Justice*, ed. Michael Zweig (Philadelphia: Temple University Press, 1991), 221–44.

24. Robert Coles and George Abbott White, "The Religion of the Privileged Ones," *Cross Currents* 31, no. 1 (1981): 7.

25. Aloysius Pieris, "Towards an Asian Theology of Liberation: Some Religio-Cultural Guidelines," *East Asian Pastoral Review* 16, no. 4 (1979): 206–30.

26. Pieris, "Christianity and Buddhism," 47–75.

27. C. Ellis Nelson, *Where Faith Begins* (Atlanta: John Knox, 1967), 43. Nowhere in the book do I find Nelson lamenting the loss of the "Protestant ethos," a loss that has led to a greater pluralism in U.S. life.

28. This is a version of an example used by Donald Evans in his marvelous reinterpretation of virtue: *Struggle and Fulfillment* (New York: Collins, 1979), 133–36. My example here remains true, even if my sense of my social location is as a "resident alien" or even an exile.

29. Nelson, *Where Faith Begins*, 184–85. This is one of many such passages in the work.

30. Here I have paraphrased in the language of discipleship a passage from Pierre Bourdieu, "The Economics of Linguistic Exchanges," *Social Science Information* 16, no. 6 (1977): 647.

Chapter 2: The Material Conditions of Our Seeing and Perceiving

1. This question comes powerfully from secular commentators, speaking from a nonreligious standpoint. See, for instance, David Denby, "Buried Alive: Our Children and the Avalanche of Crud," *New Yorker*, 15 July 1996, 48–58.

2. The words of Simeon announcing the coming birth of Jesus, in W. H. Auden, *For the Time Being* (London: Faber and Faber, 1945), 109.

3. I will say more about judgment in chapters 3 and 4. Suffice it to say the present chapter lays a foundation for making judgments about images.

4. See James Donald, review of *Privacy and Publicity: Modern Architecture as Mass Media*, by Beatriz Colomina, *Media, Culture and Society* 18 (1996): 161–63.

5. See Carl Dudley, "Using Church Images for Commitment, Conflict, and Renewal," in *Congregations: Their Power to Form and Transform*, ed. C. Ellis Nelson (Atlanta: John Knox, 1988), 89–113.

6. See David Freedberg, *The Power of Images: Studies in the History and Theory of Response* (Chicago: University of Chicago Press, 1989).

7. Ibid., 429.

8. Ibid., 2. Examples below are from pp. 3–11.

9. Ibid., 4.

10. Ibid., 5. Freedberg's comment reminds me of the following passage about the power of mimesis, or imitation, for children:

> Children are particularly vulnerable to mimetic interference. The child's confident act of imitating always runs the risk of coming up against the desires of adults, in which case his models will be transformed into fascinating obstacles. As a consequence, to the extent that in his naivety [*sic*] he is exposed to impressions from the adult world, the child is more easily and lastingly scandalized. The adult who scandalizes the child runs the risk of imprisoning him forever within the increasingly narrow circle of the model and the mimetic obstacle, the process of mutual destruction we have so often described. This process is directly opposed to the process of opening up, of welcoming others, which is life-giving.

See René Girard, *Things Hidden since the Foundation of the World*, research undertaken in collaboration with Jean-Michel Oughourlian and Guy Lefort, trans. Stephen Bann (bks. 2 and 3) and Michael Metteer (bk. 1) (Stanford: Stanford University Press, 1987), 417.

11. Freedberg, *The Power of Images*, 8–9.

12. Ibid., 17.

13. Ibid., 27.

14. Talk of the Town, *New Yorker*, 9 September 1991, 26–27.

15. Margaret Miles, *Image as Insight: Visual Understanding in Western Christianity and Secular Culture* (Boston: Beacon Press, 1985).

16. Ibid., 7.

17. For comments on the evil eye that extend and make more complex Miles's position, see Girard, *Things Hidden*, 116–17. Girard approaches the matter from the standpoint of etiology, the study of causes.

18. Catharine MacKinnon, "Pornography, Civil Rights, and Speech," *Harvard Civil Rights–Civil Liberties Law Review* 20 (1985): 3.

19. Ibid., 16–17.

20. Ibid., 18.

21. Ibid., 21.

22. For an almost comic account of the denials by studio heads and producers of the influence of their films, see Ken Auletta, "Annals of Communication: What Won't They Do?" *New Yorker*, 17 May 1993, 45–53. Pay particular attention to the passive voice, nonagent language used by Rupert Murdoch.

23. Randall Rothenberg, "The Media Business, Advertising: Panel Spurs Dispute over Alcohol Ads," *New York Times*, 2 December 1988, D14.

24. Randall Rothenberg, "Study Shows Power of Public-Service Ads," *New York Times*, 8 April 1991, D8.

25. "Advertising Unsells," *New York Times*, 8 August 1990.

26. For a critique of some naive church positions on electronic communications, see Michael Warren, "Judging the Electronic Communications Media," *Living Light* 31, no. 2 (winter 1994–95): 54–64.

27. Stuart Ewen, *All-Consuming Images: The Politics of Style in Contemporary Culture* (New York: Basic Books, 1988).

28. Ibid., 14.

29. Ibid., 19–20.

30. Ibid., 26–30, passim. Ewen's historical sources would be complemented by the first two chapters of Lester K. Little, *Religious Poverty and the Profit Economy in Medieval Europe* (Ithaca, N.Y.: Cornell University Press, 1978).

31. Ewen, *All-Consuming Images*, 39.

32. Ibid., 14.

33. Ibid., 16.

34. See Johann Baptist Metz, "Productive Noncontemporaneity," in *Observations on "The Spiritual Situation of the Age,"* ed. Jürgen Habermas (Cambridge: MIT Press, 1984), 169–77.

35. Lena Williams, "Women's Image in a Mirror: Who Defines What She Sees?" *New York Times*, 6 February 1992, A1, B7.

36. René Girard comments:

> In a world where individuals are no longer defined by the place they occupy by virtue of their birth or some other stable and arbitrary factor, the spirit of competition can never be appeased once and for all. Indeed it gets increasingly inflamed; everything rests upon comparisons that are necessarily unstable and insecure, since there are no longer any fixed points of reference.

See *Things Hidden*, 307.

37. This is one of the questions pursued by Charles Siebert, "The Cuts That Go Deeper," *New York Times Magazine*, 7 July 1996, 19–25 ff.

38. For an extensive treatment of both the role of mimesis in "hominization" and its having been overlooked, see Girard, *Things Hidden*, 3–2, 84–104. The chapters on "desire" are also worth reading.

39. David Margolick, "Ignorance of L.A. Law Is No Excuse," *New York Times*, 6 May 1990, H27, H29.

40. Readers may want to read some of the French social philosopher Jean Baudrillard's writings on this matter. See Jean Baudrillard, *Simulations* (New York: Semiotext(e), 1983); Mark Poster, ed., *Jean Baudrillard: Selected Writings* (Stanford: Stanford University Press, 1988). Poster's introduction is a helpful overview of Baudrillard's work. Another good summary of Baudrillard is Doug Kellner, "Postmodernism as Social Theory," *Theory, Culture, and Society* 5 (1988): 239–69.

41. Paul Goldberger, "25 Years of Unabashed Elitism," *New York Times*, 2 February 1992, H1, H34. See also Ada Louise Huxtable, "Inventing American Reality," *New York Review of Books*, 3 December 1992, 24–29.

42. Goldberger, "25 Years of Unabashed Elitism," H34.

43. Michael Warren, *Seeing through the Media: A Religious View of Communications and Cultural Analysis* (Valley Forge, Pa.: Trinity Press International, 1997).

44. Ewen, *All-Consuming Images*, 23.

45. This shifting of standards has a potential positive side, where former standards for talent or achievement are questioned or even overturned, allowing for a reconsideration of values. Still, my own point here is the same as Goldsmith's: the erosion of any standards for judgment except celebrity.

46. Barbara Goldsmith, "The Meaning of Celebrity," *New York Times Magazine*, 4 December 1983, 75.

47. Ibid., 76.

48. Kennedy Fraser, *The Fashionable Mind* (Boston: David R. Godine, 1985), 145–59. The title essay, placed symbolically at the very center of her book, first appeared in *New Yorker*, 13 March 1978. Citations in this paragraph are from pp. 145–46.

49. Ibid., 148. Note the similarity of Fraser's ideas with Baudrillard's comments about fashion's relation to simulation models:

> Just as the model is more real than the real..., acquiring thus a vertiginous impression of truth, the amazing aspect of fashion is that it is more beautiful than the beautiful: it is fascinating. Its seductive capacity is independent of all judgments. It exceeds the aesthetic form in the ecstatic form of unconditional metamorphosis.
>
> Whereas the aesthetic form always implies a moral distinction between the beautiful and the ugly, the ecstatic form is immoral. If there is a secret to fashion, beyond the sheer pleasures of art and taste, it is this immorality, the sovereignty of ephemeral models.

See Poster, *Jean Baudrillard*, 186.

50. Frederic Jameson, "Postmodernism, or the Cultural Logic of Late Capitalism," *New Left Review* 146 (July–August 1984): 86.

51. Ibid., 88.

52. See ibid., 89–92.

53. W. H. Auden, *For the Time Being* (London: Faber and Faber, 1945), 90.

Chapter 3: The Local Church and Its Practice of the Gospel

1. William Seth Adams, "De-coding the Obvious: Reflections on Baptismal Ministry in the Episcopal Church," *Worship* 66, no. 4 (July 1992): 327–38.

2. Impressive work is now being undertaken to examine the implicit values contained in rituals (and their multiple versions), as a kind of content analysis. See, for example, Jan Michael Joncas, "The Public Language of Ministry Revisited: *de Ordinatione Episcopi, Presbyterorum et Diaconorum* 1990," *Worship* 68, no. 5 (September 1994): 386–403; and "Solemnizing the Mystery of Wedded Love: Nuptial Blessings in the *Ordo Celebrandi Matrimonium* 1991," *Worship* 70, no. 3 (May 1996): 210–37; Catherine Vincie, "Gender Analysis and Christian Initiation," *Worship* 69, no. 6 (November 1995): 505–30.

3. Marianne Sawicki, "Recognizing the Risen Lord," *Theology Today* 44, no. 4 (1988): 441–49.

4. Storytelling, to be useful, needs to have built into it critical gospel perspectives as well as a *context* whose presuppositions provide a horizon of critique and appreciation. Stanley Hauerwas brings these critical perspectives to the fore in his conception of narrative theology and in his accounts of the faithful community. See, for example, Hauerwas's chapters "The Church as God's New Language" and "The Gesture of a Truthful Story," in *Christian Existence Today* (Durham, N.C.: Labyrinth Press, 1988); and Stanley Hauerwas and David Burrell, "From System to Story: An Alternative Pattern for Rationality in Ethics," in *Why Narrative? Readings in Narrative Theology*, ed. Stanley Hauerwas and L. Gregory Jones (Grand Rapids: Eerdmans, 1989), 158–90.

5. A sort of cousin to Nelson's book is Marianne Sawicki's examination of the conditions, both social and ecclesial, under which the ministry of the word succeeded or failed at various historical periods. See *The Gospel in History: Portrait of a Teaching Church* (New York: Paulist, 1988). A pioneering and praiseworthy effort to map the practice of some local churches, but not in my view from a sufficiently sociocritical standpoint, is Patrick J. Brennan, *Parishes That Excel: Models of Excellence in Education, Ministry, and Evangelization* (New York: Crossroad, 1992). Brennan's attention to particulars is so important that I hesitate to criticize it as not going far enough.

6. Marianne Sawicki, *Seeing the Lord: Resurrection and Early Christian Practices* (Minneapolis: Fortress, 1994). Sawicki's book is a groundbreaking work of integrative scholarship. Modern theologizing at its best, this book seems to have defied some reviewers, unable to appreciate a work leaping so nimbly and successfully across so many of the theological subdisciplines.

7. Other bodies of writing dealing with practice are ecological theology, ecofeminism, and feminism.

8. Gustavo Gutiérrez, *A Theology of Liberation*, trans. Caridad Inda and John Eagleson (Maryknoll, N.Y.: Orbis, 1973), 3.

9. Ibid., 8.

10. Ibid., 10.

11. This question is at the heart of William M. Shea's stirring analysis "Catholic Reaction to Fundamentalism," *Theological Studies* 57 (1996): 264–85.

12. Joseph Komonchak, "Ecclesiology and Social Theory," *The Thomist* 45 (1981).

13. "Here and elsewhere in this book, I step away from the using the word "praxis," at least in the sense used by Paulo Freire, with its necessary connection to theory. Neither do I delve into the history of the idea of action/praxis so helpfully explicated by Hannah Arendt in *The Human Condition* (Chicago: University of Chicago Press, 1958), 175–247, and *Between Past and Future* (New York: Penguin, 1961), 91–141. Sometimes *practice* and *praxis* are used interchangeably, as seems to be the case in Martin Jay's *The Dialectical Imagination* (Boston: Little Brown, 1973). I have selected *practice* as my category, to call attention thereby to Alisdair MacIntyre's proposals on practice in *After Virtue*, cited below. Joseph Dunne consistently uses the word "practice" in his *Back to the Rough Ground: "Phronesis" and "Techne" in Modern Philosophy and in Aristotle* (Notre Dame, Ind.: University of Notre Dame Press, 1993). Thomas McCarthy's translation of Jürgen Habermas's two-volume *Theory of Communicative Action* (Boston: Beacon Press, 1989) consistently uses the word "action" for what some might prefer to call "praxis."

14. Paul VI, *Apostolic Exhortation, "Evangelii Nuntiandi"* [On evangelization in the modern world] (Washington, D.C.: United States Catholic Conference, 1976), par. 15.

15. Ibid., par. 21.

16. Ibid., par. 76.

17. Thomas M. Finn, "Ritual Process and the Survival of Early Christianity: A Study of the Apostolic Tradition of Hippolytus," *Journal of Ritual Studies* 3, no. 1 (winter 1989): 73.

18. Here I am following a description of practice and its conditions found in Alisdair MacIntyre, *After Virtue* (Notre Dame, Ind.: University of Notre Dame Press, 1981), 175–78. The quote is on p. 177. For an application of MacIntyre's ideas to specific practices of the church, see Craig Dykstra, "Reconceiving Practice," in *Shifting Boundaries: Contextual Approaches to the Structure of Theological Education*, ed. Edward Farley and Barbara G. Wheeler (Louisville: Westminster/John Knox, 1991), 35–66.

19. The key word here is "tend." Those familiar with congregational literature know of increasing attempts to address the kind of specifics I have in mind. For example, Nelle Slater has done a wonderful case study of a particular need in a particular area met by a particular congregation but only after a series of specific struggles that pitted national policy against the gospel. See

"A Case Study of Offering Hospitality: Choosing to Be a Sanctuary Church," in *Tensions between Citizenship and Discipleship: A Case Study*, ed. Nelle G. Slater (New York: Pilgrim Press, 1989), 1–26. This entire book is a series of "studies" of the initial case from multiple points of view. The church case under review in this book followed a process remarkably like the one promoted by the Canadian Catholic bishops that I cite at the end of this chapter.

20. Pierre Bourdieu, *Outline of a Theory of Practice* (New York: Cambridge University Press, 1977), 87–88.

21. Jacques Ellul, *The Subversion of Christianity* (Grand Rapids: Eerdmans, 1986), 4.

22. Among many titles, see *Torture in Brazil*, trans. Jaime Wright, ed. Joan Dassin (New York: Vintage, 1986); Lawrence Weschler, *A Miracle, a Universe: Settling Accounts with Torturers* (New York: Penguin, 1990).

23. Here I am following the fine analysis of Roger Haight in "Critical Witness: The Question of Method," in *Faithful Witness: Foundations of Theology for Today's Church*, ed. Leo J. O'Donovan and T. Howland Sanks (New York: Crossroad, 1989), 185–204, esp. 202–4.

24. Miles Horton and Paulo Freire, *We Make the Road by Walking: Conversations on Education and Social Change*, ed. Brenda Bell et al. (Philadelphia: Temple University Press, 1990), 77.

25. Gustavo Gutiérrez, *The Power of the Poor in History* (Maryknoll, N.Y.: Orbis, 1983), 17.

26. Aloysius Pieris, "Christianity and Buddhism in Core-to-Core Dialogue," *Cross Currents* 37, no. 1 (spring 1987): 48. For a version of this essay, see Aloysius Pieris, *Love Meets Wisdom: A Christian Experience of Buddhism* (Maryknoll, N.Y.: Orbis, 1988), chap. 10.

27. Pieris, "Christianity and Buddhism in Core-to-Core Dialogue," 48.

28. Ibid., 52. In another essay Pieris explains the same phenomenon:

> In the formative centuries of Christian monasticism, the gnostic spirituality of the non-Christian gradually filtered into the agapeic religiosity of the monks. While this symbiosis was taking place in the silence of the monastic cells, the academic theologians of the church were busy experimenting with the legal language of the Latins and the philosophical thought of the Greeks to make "precision instruments" that would enable the human mind to fathom the Mystery of Christ, thus producing a vast corpus of theological literature that paved the way for christological dogmas and, centuries later, *for an overgrowth of scholasticism* [emphasis added].

See Aloysius Pieris, "Western Models of Inculturation: How Far Are They Applicable in Non-Semitic Asia?" in *An Asian Theology of Liberation* (Maryknoll, N.Y.: Orbis, 1988), 56.

29. Tertullian, "On Penitence," in *Treatises on Penance*, trans. W. Le Saint (Westminster, Md.: Newman, 1959), 24–26.

30. Regis Duffy, "Liturgical Catechesis: Catechumenal Models" (unpublished paper given as the Mary Charles Bryce Lecture, Catholic University, Washington, D.C., April 1983).

31. Here I am following Pieris in *Love Meets Wisdom*, 17–42, esp. 18–23. In *The Liberation of Dogma* (Maryknoll, N.Y.: Orbis, 1992), Juan Luis Segundo, while never making Pieris's precise point, obliquely but insistently deals with the underlying issue of how the inner life of the ecclesia is communicated. See pp. 117–58.

32. Some particular examples: Edward Farley, "Theology and Practice outside the Clerical Paradigm," in *Practical Theology*, ed. Don S. Browning (San Francisco: Harper and Row, 1983), 21–41; *Theologia: The Fragmentation and Unity of Theological Education* (Philadelphia: Fortress, 1983), esp. chap. 4, "Schleiermacher and the Beginning of the Encyclopedia Movement," pp. 73–94 but also pp. 127–34; "Interpreting Situations: An Inquiry into the Nature of Practical Theology," in *Formation and Reflection: The Promise of Practical Theology*, ed. Lewis S. Mudge and James N. Poling (Philadelphia: Fortress, 1987), 1–35.

For Farley on the materiality of ecclesial life, see *Ecclesial Reflection: An Anatomy of Theological Method* (Philadelphia: Fortress, 1982), esp. chaps. 9–11.

33. Pieris, "Christianity and Buddhism," 73.

34. Ibid.

35. Daniel Levinson, *The Seasons of a Man's Life* (New York: Knopf, 1978), 41–42.

36. Ibid., 43.

37. Chris O'Sullivan, "Campus Rape Is Usually Fraternity-Related" (letter to the editor), *New York Times*, 5 December 1990, A26. See also Gerald Eskenazi, "The Male Athlete and Sexual Assault," *New York Times*, 3 June 1990, L1, L4.

38. For evidence of this claim, see Shea, "Catholic Reaction to Fundamentalism."

39. Cited in Harry Emerson Fosdick, *Great Voices of the Reformation: An Anthology* (New York: Modern Library, 1952), xx–xxi.

40. I realize the Reformation's complexity is such that it cannot be reduced to this single aspect.

41. See the description of this process in Gregory Baum, *Truth beyond Relativism: Karl Mannheim's Sociology of Knowledge* (Milwaukee: Marquette University Press, 1977), 60–62.

42. Cut-and-dried formulas also tend to be reductionistic, even trivializing the open-endedness of the gospel's demands. The lists of sins offered for preparation for the sacrament of penance in Roman Catholic devotional books, even for years after Vatican II, though they do call attention to concrete behavior, reduce the behavior to negative acts easily numbered for the sake of accuracy. This kind of limiting has a long history, as can be seen in the following handbook for determining both sins and the penalties needing to be fulfilled before they could be pardoned: "Haltigar: Prescriptions for Sins," in *Pastoral Care in*

Historical Perspective, ed. Charles Jaeckle and William A. Clebsch, eds. (New York: Jason Aronson, 1975), 148–64.

43. See the helpful comments on "discourse ethics" in Paul Lakeland, *Theology and Critical Theory* (Nashville: Abingdon, 1990), 174–207.

44. Dialogue is not my main theme in this chapter but will be in chapter 5. I agree with Johannes Metz that religious people have to enter a "hermeneutical culture" marked by respectful dialogue ("encountering others in their otherness") toward coping with human problems. Johann Baptist Metz, "With the Eyes of a European Theologian," in *The Voice of the Victims,* ed. L. Boff and V. Elizondo, Concilium Series (London: SCM, 1990), 113–19.

45. I realize how the actual making of a decision in many cases is not just a matter of using ultimate norms. The decision affects usually a person's response to a particular situation that may not be resolvable by ultimate norms only. A person may recognize particular features of the situation that, along with the norms, guide the decision. See Isaiah Berlin, "On Political Judgment," *New York Review,* 3 October 1996, 26–30.

46. Among Roman Catholics, Francis Schüssler Fiorenza's *Foundational Theology* (New York: Crossroad, 1984) raises important issues related to practice, as does Edward Schillebeeckx in his more recent *Church: The Human Story of God* (New York: Crossroad, 1990); also, *Faithful Witness,* already cited in n. 23. In the writings of the most philosophical of modern Roman Catholic theologians, Karl Rahner, I find practice a seminal concern.

47. My point here is similar to Edith Wyschogrod's argument against moral theory as basically failing to achieve its predetermined goal of transforming moral conduct. Her examination of saints and saintliness chooses instead to examine life histories and recover from them their "exhortative force" and their patterns of practice. See *Saints and Postmodernism: Revisioning Moral Philosophy* (Chicago: University of Chicago Press, 1990), xiii–xxvii.

48. Sawicki, *Seeing the Lord,* 301–36.

49. A particularly illuminating case study is Slater, *Tensions between Citizenship and Discipleship.* A sort of master set of case studies and an orientation to them is James P. Wind and James W. Lewis, *American Congregations,* 2 vols. (Chicago: University of Chicago Press, 1994).

50. See n. 5 above.

51. See n. 32.

52. Canadian Conference of Catholic Bishops, *Ethical Choices and Political Challenges: Ethical Reflections on the Future of Canada's Socio-Economic Order* (Ottawa: Canadian Conference of Catholic Bishops, 1984), 2.

53. See Nelle G. Slater, "A Case Study of Offering Hospitality," in *Tensions between Citizenship and Discipleship,* for an account of a church that followed a transformative process very much like the one outlined in these steps.

54. Roger Haight writes:

> Christian spirituality means living out . . . vision in action. When spirituality is thus conceived as human action, one has the basis for an objective

consideration of the adequacy of the method of theology. Christian life and action unfold within the church in its mission to the world and within the world itself.

See "Critical Witness," 203.

Chapter 4: How We Speak in the Church

1. John Paul II, discourse to the bishops of Zaire, 12 April 1983, no. 5: *Acta apostolicae sedis* 75 (1983): 620.]

2. In connection with this point about passivity, see Francis Schüssler Fiorenza, "Theory and Practice: Theological Education as a Reconstructive, Hermeneutical, and Practical Task," *Theological Education Supplement* (1987): 122.

3. The houseguest metaphor was suggested by Maire Hunt of Sligo, Ireland, when she was a graduate student at St. John's University. Her insight was echoed sometime later in Gary David Comstock, "The Houseguesting of Gay Scholars," *Council of Societies for the Study of Religion Bulletin* 23, no. 2 (April 1994): 35–37.

4. See the interesting use of this metaphor in Walter Brueggemann, "Textuality in the Church," in *Tensions between Citizenship and Discipleship: A Case Study*, ed. Nelle G. Slater (New York: Pilgrim Press, 1989), 48–68.

5. For a broader perspective on my claim here, see Francis Schüssler Fiorenza, "Theological and Religious Studies: The Contest of the Faculties," in *Shifting Boundaries: Contextual Approaches to the Structure of Theological Education*, ed. Edward Farley and Barbara G. Wheeler (Louisville: Westminster/John Knox, 1991), 141–42.

6. In 1979, Mary Collins published what appeared to me a groundbreaking critical examination of liturgical rites, suggesting the critical task for liturgical theology is to ask whether the faith vision celebrated in liturgy is adequate. See "Critical Questions for Liturgical Theology," *Worship* 53, no. 4 (1979): 302–17.

There are other metaphors of visibility to complement mine. Edward Farley uses "portrait," which is a rendition of reality bringing out features present but not obvious. See chapter 9, "Theological Portraiture," and other sections of his *Ecclesial Reflection: An Anatomy of Theological Method* (Philadelphia: Fortress, 1982).

7. Some will rightly point to the idealized character of some New Testament accounts of life in the earliest communities. Overall, the multiple "fissures" exposing deep struggles in these New Testament communities provide a helpful counterweight to idealizations.

8. Here I follow the argument of Lester K. Little, "Evangelical Poverty, the New Money Economy, and Violence," in *Poverty in the Middle Ages*, ed. David Flood (Werl/Westfl., Germany: Dietrich-Coelde-Verlag, 1975), 11–26, esp. 21–22.

9. David N. Power, "Households of Faith in the Coming Church," *Worship* 57, no. 3 (May 1983): 238.

10. See Lester K. Little, *Religious Poverty and the Profit Economy in Medieval Europe* (Ithaca, N.Y.: Cornell University Press, 1978), 200–217.

11. Though the flourishing of laypeople in full-time parish ministry might seem to contradict my position here, I have found it confirmed by conversations with these same ministers.

12. This matter of participation is complex, as became clear to me from reading Eamon Duffy's, *The Stripping of the Altars: Traditional Religion in England 1400–1580* (New Haven: Yale University Press, 1992). Duffy outlines how much lay participation expanded, both in various liturgical rituals and in their spillover into the various dramatic forms of mystery plays and the like. In certain feasts and liturgical sequences there evolved a highly participatory character of bodily movement, gestures, spoken and sung participation. But still, this participation did not have the character of critical agency. Alas, Duffy himself overlooks what seems to me the clear matters of social class underlying the life patterns he so astutely surfaces. His purpose, in what turns out to be as much polemic as history, is to praise pre-Reformation "traditional religion," to the point of refusing to critique it. Similarly, almost all reviews of Duffy's book overlook how deeply class and status were reflected in this "traditional religion." See pp. 11–29.

13. Pierre Bourdieu, "The Economics of Linguistic Exchanges," *Social Science Information* 16, no. 6 (1977): 647. The full paragraph preceding this one is my paraphrase of sections of Bourdieu's article. Bourdieu gets at the question of forming a community of discourse, instead of a social situation marked by manifestos, pronouncements, and other elocutions from on high. The question of a community of moral discourse as a common struggle toward truth and fidelity is one I find missing in John Paul II's *Splendor Veritatis* (1993).

14. Once put this way, the question of rhetorical skills — the ability to express effectively one's position — raises a host of other but related questions about speech and power.

15. Among the more powerful exceptions to my claim here is Rebecca Chopp, *The Power to Speak: Feminism, Language, God* (New York: Crossroad, 1989).

In his essay cited here, Bourdieu makes a comment of interest to educators and pastoral ministers, including liturgists. He contrasts prophetic discourse and institutionalized discourse: "In assuming the fact of communication, the linguist brackets the social conditions of the possibility of establishing discourse, which come to light, for example, in the case of prophetic discourse — as opposed to institutionalized discourse, the lecture or sermon, which presupposes pedagogic or sacerdotal authority." See "The Economics of Linguistic Exchanges," 649.

16. See the careful, but indirect, way Segundo, writing as a catechist, deals with this problem of participation in Juan Luis Segundo, "A Foreword That Isn't," chap. 1 in *The Liberation of Dogma* (Maryknoll, N.Y.: Orbis, 1992), 1–15.

17. Two recent examples of such study are Eamon Duffy, *The Stripping of the Altars*, and Gerard S. Sloyan, "Piety Centered on Jesus' Sufferings and Some Ec-

centric Christian Understandings of the Mystery of Calvary," *Worship* 67, no. 2 (March 1993): 98–123.

18. In this section I am following the argument in David N. Power, "Power and Authority in Early Christian Centuries," in *That They Might Live: Power, Empowerment, and Leadership in the Church*, ed. Michael Downey (New York: Crossroad, 1991), 25–38. I am aware, as Power himself surely is, how recent scholarship has exposed issues of hidden power and silencing in the canonical texts that have come down to us. Only some accounts survived, those of elites able to write, while others were in various ways suppressed or lost. The canonical texts reflect a minority and perhaps a tiny one, among the Jesus movements.

19. The varieties would include those that cracked the hard shell of patriarchy to give women equal voice and those that did not.

20. Power, "Power and Authority," 30.

21. For a glimpse of how the erosion of this understanding of God's power works in the life of the ordinary Christian, see William Seth Adams's study of the rites of baptism and ordination in the Episcopal Church: "De-coding the Obvious: Reflections on Baptismal Ministry in the Episcopal Church," *Worship* 66, no. 4 (July 1992): 327–38.

22. In *Saints and Postmodernism* (Chicago: University of Chicago Press, 1990) Edith Wyschogrod defines saintliness from a secular point of view as a way of giving attention to persons who put aside personal comfort to side with misery. In my view her book and Power's essay are related.

23. See the issues of the *Catholic Worker* for any single year since its inception for examples. I presume other examples can be found in the letters written by provincial superiors and circulated to province members in religious orders.

24. Power, "Power and Authority," 37.

25. In his essay, "Le Langage Autorisé: note sur les conditions sociales de l'efficacité du discours rituel," *Actes de la recherche en sciences sociales* (November 1975): 183–90, Bourdieu raises questions some readers will find provocative about the procedures used to establish the authority of ritual. Though at the end Bourdieu seems to be against liturgical change, this essay's main argument remains an important companion piece to "The Economics of Linguistic Exchanges" cited above in n. 13.

26. Some are alarmed that the so-called canon of culturally respectable texts (named "culture" by some) may be changed to new ones, texts they have not studied — and therefore not appreciated. The literary traditions of recognized power in the past — those same traditions that served so well one set of interests and one base of power — lose their hegemony by now being set as one tradition among many worthwhile ones. Some claim the issue is "culture," but the real issue has to do with whose voices are worthy of being heard.

27. Here I am following the analysis used in Bob Hurd, "Liturgy and Empowerment: The Restoration of the Liturgical Assembly," in *That They Might Live: Power, Empowerment, and Leadership in the Church*, ed. Michael Downey (New York: Crossroad, 1991), 130–44. Compare Hurd's treatment of assem-

bly with the following one, which for all practical purposes ignores the issue of power and speech: Catherine Vincie, "The Liturgical Assembly: Review and Reassessment," *Worship* 67, no. 2 (1993): 123–44.

28. Hurd, "Liturgy and Empowerment," 131.

29. This statement is not my own, but I am unable to find its source. It most likely occurs in the writings of Pierre Bourdieu. The *idea*, however, informs every line of Shoshana Felman, "Psychoanalysis and Education: Teaching Terminable and Interminable," *Yale French Studies* 63 (1982): 21–44.

30. Chopp, *The Power to Speak*, 89. Richard Bernstein offers helpful reflections on participation in his examination of Hannah Arendt's position on practical discourse. See *Beyond Objectivism and Relativism: Science, Hermeneutics, and Praxis* (Philadelphia: University of Pennsylvania Press, 1983), 207–15.

31. This point is brought out in some detail by Joseph Komonchak in "Clergy, Laity, and the Church's Mission in the World," *The Jurist* 41 (1981): 422–47, esp. 439–42.

32. Stanley Hauerwas (and David Burrell), "From System to Story: An Alternative Pattern for Rationality in Ethics," in *Why Narrative? Readings in Narrative Theology*, ed. Stanley Hauerwas and L. Gregory Jones (Grand Rapids: Eerdmans, 1989), 168. This same point is made in various places in Darrell J. Fasching, *Narrative Theology after Auschwitz: From Alienation to Ethics* (Minneapolis: Fortress, 1992).

33. Francis Schüssler Fiorenza has written extensively on the faith community as a zone of hermeneutical reflection. For a more recent account of his provocative thinking, see Francis Schüssler Fiorenza, "The Crisis of Hermeneutics and Christian Theology," in *Theology at the End of Modernity*, ed. Sheila Greeve Davaney (Philadelphia: Trinity Press International, 1991), 117–40. Another helpful resource is Paul Lakeland, *Theology and Critical Theory: The Discourse of the Church* (Nashville: Abingdon, 1990), esp. chaps. 4–6.

34. Fiorenza, "Crisis of Hermeneutics and Christian Theology," 133–34.

35. Ibid., 135–36. So many important works make this point that I here name the one many readers might overlook: Wyschogrod's *Saints and Postmodernism*.

36. See C. Ellis Nelson, "Some Educational Aspects of Conflict," in *Tensions between Citizenship and Discipleship: A Case Study*, ed. Nelle G. Slater (New York: Pilgrim Press, 1989), 195–218.

37. Joshua Meyrowitz, *No Sense of Place: The Impact of Electronic Media on Social Behavior* (New York: Oxford University Press, 1986), 309.

38. See Gregory Baum, "The Dumont Report," in *The Tabu of Democracy within the Church*, ed. James Provost and Knut Walf, Concilium Series (London: SCM, 1992), 106–13.

39. For a well-stated overview, see Ladislaus Orsy, "New Era of Participation in Church Life," *Origins* 17, no. 46 (28 April 1988): 796–800.

40. Here I have in mind Ricoeur's *Oneself as Another* (Chicago: University of Chicago Press, 1992), with its recurring emphasis on person as agent and the

importance of agency. I have become aware of how seminal a place agency has in my own *Seeing through the Media.*

41. A compelling recent treatment of God's ecclesial agency is Reinhard Hutter, "Ecclesial Ethics, the Church's Vocation, and Paraclesis," *Pro Ecclesia* 2, no. 4 (fall 1993): 433–50. See especially the section "Ecclesial Ethics as Paraclesis" on pp. 439–43. In another place, Hutter again emphasizes that in ecclesial action the focus of agency is not on the self but on God. It is not that the self is not an agent but that fidelity to God is at the center of the self's agency. See Hutter, "The Church as Public: Dogma, Practice, and the Holy Spirit," *Pro Ecclesia* 3, no. 3 (summer 1994): 334–61.

42. Søren Kierkegaard, *Purity of Heart Is to Will One Thing: Spiritual Preparation for the Office of Confession,* trans. Douglas V. Steere (New York: Harper Torchbooks, 1956), 177–84. This passage occurs in the first of a series of three chapters, the title of each of which begins with the phrase, "What then must I do?" They are about agency. Donald Kraus called my attention to this text.

The best recent theological treatment of God's agency I have found is Reinhard Hutter's "Ecclesial Ethics."

43. Ben H. Bagdikian, "The Lords of the Global Village," *The Nation,* 12 June 1989, 819.

44. Stanley Aronowitz and Henry Giroux, *Education under Siege* (Amherst, Mass.: Bergin and Garvey, 1985), 51. My assumption is that this passage was written by Aronowitz.

45. Here I refer to Alain Touraine's *Return of the Actor: Social Theory in Post-industrial Society,* trans. Myrna Godzich (Minneapolis: University of Minnesota Press, 1988). Especially helpful in this volume is the introduction by Stanley Aronowitz.

46. I have in mind the work of Mary Collins, Rebecca Chopp, Nelle Slater, and Sheila Greeve Davaney cited in this chapter, but also those like Elisabeth Schüssler Fiorenza in her efforts to reclaim the muted voices from Scripture and Elizabeth Johnson and Sallie McFague for their work of questioning exclusivist metaphors and of doing theology from inclusive approaches. See also Marianne Sawicki's move away from incursive theological metaphors in favor of nonincursive or "intertextual" approaches in *Seeing the Lord: Resurrection and Early Christian Practices* (Minneapolis: Fortress, 1994).

Religious-education professors like Joan Marie Smith, Gloria Durka, Maria Harris, and Mary Elizabeth Moore have helped their peers become more aware of full participation at national meetings by doing on-the-spot discourse analysis.

47. I am struck with how much of Dykstra's "Reconceiving Practice" (in *Shifting Boundaries: Contextual Approaches to the Structure of Theological Education,* ed. Edward Farley and Barbara G. Wheeler [Louisville: Westminster/John Knox, 1991], 35–66) focuses on the primal practice of speaking.

48. The notion of agency — without much explicit use of the word — suffuses the approach to the local church of C. Ellis Nelson in *How Faith Ma-*

tures (Louisville: Westminster/John Knox, 1989). See especially the last section, "Experiential Religion," 151–230.

49. Chopp, *The Power to Speak*, 8.

50. With convincing eloquence Francis Schüssler Fiorenza makes this same point in "Crisis of Hermeneutics and Christian Theology," 140.

Chapter 5: Life Structure, or the Material Conditions of Living

1. See, for example, Michael Warren, *Youth, Gospel, Liberation*, 3d ed. (Dublin: Veritas, 1998), especially chaps. 12 and 13.

2. James Atlas, "Beyond Demographics: How Madison Avenue Knows Who You Are and What You Want," *Atlantic Monthly*, October 1984, 51.

3. Ibid., 58.

4. See Jürgen Habermas, *The Theory of Communicative Action*, vol. 2, *Lifeworld and System: A Critique of Functionalist Reason*, trans. Thomas McCarthy (Boston: Beacon Press, 1989), 323–26.

5. A few years ago I did an informal survey of summer programs of spiritual renewal in the United States and Ireland and found that most of them described spirituality in terms of prayer and worship, with no indication in the printed material that retreatants were going to consider their wider patterns of engagement with the world. Prayer seemed to define a way of turning to the self and away from the particular material conditions of one's wider life. I presume an updated survey would disclose the same patterns. An exception to this tendency would be the Ignatian Exercises, which get at the embodiment of discipleship in particular circumstances.

6. See for example the statistically sophisticated studies of "time use" in F. Thomas Juster and Frank P. Stafford, eds., *Time, Goods, and Well-Being* (Ann Arbor: University of Michigan Institute for Social Research, 1985). Of particular use to marketing people — but also to the churches — are Martha S. Hill, "Patterns of Time Use," 133–76; and John P. Robinson, "Changes in Time Use: An Historical Overview," 289–311. Robinson's examination of shifts in time use for the following categories — work, family care, sleep, personal care, and free time — offers data worth pondering, such as, "In terms of overall shift in free-time activities, however, the most impressive 1965–75 shift occurs for television" (p. 300).

7. Roger Haight, "Critical Witness: The Question of Method," in *Faithful Witness: Foundations of Theology for Today's Church*, ed. Leo J. O'Donovan and T. Howland Sanks (New York: Crossroad, 1989), 191. The same point is made often in the writings of Francis Schüssler Fiorenza.

8. See Pierre Bourdieu, *Distinction: A Social Critique of the Judgement of Taste* (Cambridge: Harvard University Press, 1984), 101. Here I paraphrase the sense of his argument, found in so many of his writings.

9. Bourdieu uses the word "practice" very deliberately. In his own words,

I have never used the concept of praxis which, at least in French, tends to create the impression of something pompously theoretical — which is pretty paradoxical — and makes me think of trendy Marxism, the young Marx, the Frankfurt School, Yugoslav Marxism....I've always talked, quite simply, about practice.

See Pierre Bourdieu, *In Other Words: Essays towards a Reflexive Sociology*, trans. Matthew Adamson (Stanford: Stanford University Press, 1990), 22.

10. Pierre Bourdieu, *Outline of a Theory of Practice* (New York: Cambridge University Press, 1977), 80. I have found very little about habitat in Bourdieu's writings to which I have had access; his entire focus seems to be on the habitus.

11. Among the many places in his writings where Bourdieu uses this metaphor of the game, see *The Logic of Practice*, trans. Richard Nice (Stanford: Stanford University Press, 1990), chap. 4, "Belief and the Body," pp. 66–67.

12. Ibid., 68–69. Bourdieu seems to agree with Charles Sanders Peirce's often-quoted description of a belief as that which directs and becomes embedded in action: "The essence of belief is the establishment of a habit, and different beliefs are distinguished by the different modes of action to which they give rise." See Charles Sanders Peirce, "How to Make Our Ideas Clear," in *Writings of Charles Sanders Peirce: A Chronological Edition*, vol. 3 (1872–78) (Bloomington: Indiana University Press, 1986), 263–64.

13. Bourdieu, *Theory of Practice*, 94.

14. My analogy here is not meant to imply the tightrope walker is not "in the world" but somehow above it. If she walks the rope as a public exercise of her skill, she is as much a part of the public mix as the one ambling down the street.

15. Bourdieu, *Theory of Practice*, 87.

16. Ibid., 81–82. Bourdieu seems to assume that social class is tightly tied to economic status. However consumerist capitalism's way of conceiving money tends to blur distinctions among classes and even among economic levels, as can be seen in the way some of the VALS categories cut across or even ignore lines of class and income. The VALS analysts' concern with the decisions people actually make in their daily lives is close to my own concern here.

17. Ibid., 85–86. Also, see Bourdieu, *Distinction*, 193–97, for his comparison of working-class meals and those of the middle class.

In my view Bourdieu here seems to oversimplify social reality, though possibly he does so for heuristic and rhetorical purposes. While his overall point about economic position and social class having their agenda is important (especially for those concerned for justice), he seems to ignore the work of particular social agents skillfully using electronic communications to orchestrate a desire for goods and their decisive influence on human perception and attitudes.

18. Bourdieu, *Theory of Practice*, 169.

19. Ibid. Here and below I am following Bourdieu's argument on this page.

20. Ibid.

21. Gregory Baum sketches this same process well:

[I]n every society there are dominant classes and authoritative institutions, upheld by a culture produced by them, — and there are lower and marginal strata. Every society is stratified. From the lower strata the society presents an image that is quite different from its self-understanding produced and communicated by the dominant culture. From the lower strata become visible the weaknesses, injustices and contradictions that remain hidden from those identified with the dominant structures. The modes of thought accepted by a culture and the social virtues recommended by it have an ugly underside that is discoverable by the inferiorized groups. People of the lower strata express their protest against the world that oppresses them in religious or secular symbols of various kinds, and when they gain access to learning they are able to develop modes of thought and advocate values that transcend the dominant culture. Culturally transcendent perceptions usually emerge in marginal movements, like the movement started by Jesus of Nazareth, that are repudiated by the defenders of the dominant structures and survive only by remaining partially underground. Transcendence does not emerge in the offices of tenured professors nor does it arise in chancery offices. Transcendence has always demanded a price, like the pearl of great value.

See Gregory Baum, *Truth beyond Relativism: Karl Mannheim's Sociology of Knowledge* (Milwaukee: Marquette University Press, 1977), 60–62.

22. Donald Kraus, after reading an early version of this chapter, warned me about oversimplifying here. Possibly the highest internalization of norms leads not so much to conscious judgments but to implicit judgments. Not all discernment is conscious. A young child may show an astonishing internalization of norms of goodness and consequent action.

In *Saints and Postmodernism: Revisioning Moral Philosophy* (Chicago: University of Chicago Press, 1990), Edith Wyschogrod examines and prizes the nonlogical judgments of virtuoso goodness. My concern here is the possibility that religious people can make habitual judgments that contradict the norms of their sacred texts.

23. See, for example, the careful description of the normative interpretive activity in early Christian "desert" monasticism in Douglas Burton-Christie, *The Word in the Desert: Scripture and the Quest for Holiness in Early Christian Monasticism* (New York: Oxford University Press, 1993). This study has interesting implications for the place of religious groups within a wider culture.

24. Here I am touching on an important matter outside the scope of this chapter: norms themselves falling under norms. Liberative practice tests or helps disclose the character of the textual norm. Also within sacred texts are contradictory norms needing examination as well as norms at different levels of normativity, with some overriding others. Sexism and other pathologies implicit in sacred texts need to be critiqued by the text's own deepest witness. See Sandra Schneiders, "Living Word or Dead(ly) Letters: The Encounter between the New Testament and Contemporary Experience," *Catholic Theological Society*

of *America Proceedings* 47 (1992): 45–60; and "Scripture as the Word of God," *Princeton Seminary Review* 14, no. 1 (February 1993): 18–35.

25. Justus Buchler begins his 1961 book on judgment with a description of what he calls "proception," a way of being in the world that is in large part outside of awareness. Proception is at least a cousin to Bourdieu's habitus. See Justus Buchler, *Toward a General Theory of Human Judgment* (New York: Columbia University Press, 1961), 6–10.

26. Some might suspect the stress here on intentionality and normativity has about it an irreligious hint of instrumental rationality and its passion for control. While I am trying to get at matters religious people should be able to bring to discourse, I understand the human rooted in dimensions of the nonrational and unsayable. The issue here is not rational control but fidelity.

27. Daniel Levinson's *The Seasons of a Man's Life* (New York: Knopf, 1978) has been followed up with the posthumous publication *The Seasons of a Woman's Life*, written in collaboration with Judy D. Levinson (New York: Knopf, 1996). The more recent book has additional reflections on life structure.

28. The VALS "lifestyles" typology seems to be misnamed since it describes life structures more than lifestyles.

29. C. Ellis Nelson, *Where Faith Begins* (Atlanta: John Knox Press, 1967), 189.

30. See Elizabeth Grosz, *Sexual Subversions: Three French Feminists* (Boston: Allen and Unwin, 1989), 39–55, esp. 52–54.

31. Habermas, *Lifeworld and System*, 172.

32. Ibid., 173.

33. Francis Schüssler Fiorenza, "Foundational Theology and Theological Education," *Theological Education* (spring 1984): 119.

34. See John Howard Yoder's examination of the process of allowing every prophetic voice to be heard and every witness evaluated in what he calls radical Protestantism: "The Hermeneutics of Peoplehood," in *The Priestly Kingdom: Social Ethics as Gospel* (Notre Dame, Ind.: University of Notre Dame Press, 1984), 15–45. Some of the characteristics of what Yoder calls the "free churches" need to be recovered by all local churches today.

35. See the pastoral methodology of the Canadian Catholic Bishops, cited on p. 72.

36. Some of the guidelines I have in mind are the following series of articles by Francis Schüssler Fiorenza: "Foundations of Theology: A Community's Tradition of Discourse and Practice," *Catholic Theological Society of America Proceedings* 41 (1986): 107–34; "Theory and Practice: Theological Education as a Reconstructive, Hermeneutical, and Practical Task," *Theological Education Supplement* (1987): 113–41; "The Church as a Community of Interpretation: Political Theology between Discourse Ethics and Hermeneutical Reconstruction," in *Habermas, Modernity, and Public Theology*, ed. Don S. Browning and Francis Schüssler Fiorenza (New York: Crossroad, 1992), 66–91. Also Edward Farley, "Interpreting Situations: An Inquiry into the Nature of Practical Theology," in *Formation and Reflection: The Promise of Practical Theology*, ed. Lewis S.

Mudge and James N. Poling (Philadelphia: Fortress, 1987), 1–35; and "Theology and Practice outside the Clerical Paradigm," in *Practical Theology*, ed. Don S. Browning (San Francisco: Harper and Row, 1983), 21–41; Rebecca Chopp, *The Power to Speak: Feminism, Language, God* (New York: Crossroad, 1989); Sharon D. Welch, *A Feminist Ethic of Risk* (Minneapolis: Augsburg, 1990).

37. Francis Schüssler Fiorenza, "The Crisis of Hermeneutics and Christian Theology," in *Theology at the End of Modernity*, ed. Sheila Greeve Davaney (Philadelphia: Trinity Press International, 1991), 117–40.

38. Here I have paraphrased comments in Fiorenza, "Theory and Practice," 117.

39. I am summarizing a powerful passage in Susan Brooks Thistlethwaite and Mary Potter Engel, eds., introduction to *Lift Every Voice: Constructing Christian Theologies from the Underside* (San Francisco: HarperSanFrancisco, 1990), 1–2.

Chapter 6: Spirit Resonance

1. Bernard Lonergan, "The Transition from a Classicist Worldview to Historical-Mindedness," in *A Second Collection*, ed. William Ryan and Bernard Tyrrell (Philadelphia: Westminster, 1974), 7–8. Another version of the same idea is also found in "The Ongoing Genesis of Methods," *Studies in Religion* 6, no. 4 (1976–77): 341–55.

2. Jerome Bruner, *The Culture of Education* (Cambridge: Harvard University Press, 1996), esp. chap. 8, "Knowing as Doing," pp. 150–59. See also Clifford Geertz's review of this book, "Learning with Bruner," *New York Review of Books*, 10 April 1997, 22–24.

3. See *The Spiritual Exercises of Ignatius Loyola*, trans. Louis J. Puhl (Westminster, Md.: Newman, 1951).

4. Malcolm Gladwell, "A Reporter at Large: The Science of Shopping," *New Yorker*, 4 November 1996: 66–75. Examples abound for how consumerist capitalism takes seriously various "segments" of the consumer population, like youth, while the churches are basically not paying anything like the same kind of attention to what young people are actually living. See, for example, Robin Pogrebin, "Magazines Learning to Take Not-so-Clueless (and Monied) Teenagers More Seriously," *New York Times*, 4 November 1996, D8.

5. See Pierre Bourdieu, *In Other Words: Essays towards a Reflexive Sociology*, trans. Matthew Adamson (Stanford: Stanford University Press, 1990), 22. I have already alluded to these uses of practice in chap. 5, n. 9. Though the Marxist use of "praxis" has real value, I have avoided it in this book in order that readers not pigeonhole my use of "practice" as something they already grasp well. I have been seeking a rethinking or a reknowing of the problem of practice.

6. Alisdair MacIntyre, *After Virtue* (Notre Dame, Ind.: University of Notre Dame Press, 1981), 175. In this section I am using MacIntyre and the following two sources: Joseph Dunne, "What's the Good of Education?" in *Partnership and the Benefits of Learning: A Symposium on Philosophical Issues of Educational Policy*, ed. Padraig Hogan (Maynooth, Ireland: Educational Studies Association

of Ireland, 1995), 60–82 and 157–59; Craig Dykstra, "Reconceiving Practice," in *Shifting Boundaries: Contextual Approaches to the Structure of Theological Education*, ed. Edward Farley and Barbara G. Wheeler (Louisville: Westminster/John Knox, 1991), 35–66.

7. This is the underlying point of two chapters in my *Faith, Culture, and the Worshiping Community: Shaping the Practice of the Local Church* (Washington, D.C.: Pastoral Press, 1993): "Catechesis and the Captive Audiences," pp. 37–52, and "The Catechumen in the Kitchen," pp. 89–105.

8. For an example of these goods, see Stanley Hauerwas's account of his father's life as a bricklayer and mason, "All We Have Is the Church," in *In Good Company: The Church as Polis* (Notre Dame, Ind.: University of Notre Dame Press, 1995), 33–49.

9. See Kennedy Fraser, "Piper Pipe That Song Again," review of *Blake*, by Peter Ackroyd, *New Yorker*, 27 May 1996, 126–31.

10. For a compelling reflection on this matter, see Aloysius Pieris, "To Be Poor as Jesus Was Poor," *The Way* (July 1984): 186–97.

11. Dunne, "What's the Good of Education?" 75.

12. Felix Dupanloup, *The Ministry of Catechizing* (London and Sydney: Griffith, Farran, Okeden and Welsh, 1890), 548–49. See also the following pages to 553.

13. Ibid., 553.

14. The matter of communion goes beyond fellowship within a single local church or a single denomination. William Shea warns cogently against almost nasty attitudes to Christians with whom we do not see eye-to-eye doctrinally. See William M. Shea, "Catholic Reaction to Fundamentalism," *Theological Studies* 57 (1996): 264–85.

15. In thinking about this complex matter, I have found much wisdom in Parker Palmer, *The Company of Strangers: Christians and the Renewal of America's Public Life* (New York: Crossroad, 1983).

16. See the wonderful but little-publicized *Guide for Catechists*, issued by the Roman Congregation for the Evangelization of Peoples in 1993. This document can be found in Michael Warren, *Sourcebook for Modern Catechetics*, vol. 2 (Winona, Minn.: St. Mary's Press, 1997).

17. See the extraordinary 1996 document issued by the Pontifical Council for the Family: "Preparation for the Sacrament of Marriage," *Origins* 26, no. 7 (4 July 1996): 97, 99–109.

18. This is what is most wonderful about Patrick Brennan's book *Parishes That Excel*, which I have critiqued elsewhere in this book. See *Parishes That Excel: Models of Excellence in Education, Ministry, and Evangelization* (New York: Crossroad, 1992).

Bibliography

Abbott, W. M., and J. Gallagher, eds. *The Documents of Vatican II*. New York: Association Press, 1966.

Adams, William Seth. "De-coding the Obvious: Reflections on Baptismal Ministry in the Episcopal Church." *Worship* 66, no. 4 (July 1992): 327–38.

Arendt, Hannah. *Between Past and Future*. New York: Penguin, 1977.

———. *The Human Condition*. Chicago: University of Chicago Press, 1958.

Aronowicz, Annette. "Translator's Introduction" to *Nine Talmudic Readings*, by Emmanuel Lévinas. Bloomington: University of Indiana Press, 1994.

Aronowitz, Stanley, and Henry Giroux. *Education under Siege*. Amherst, Mass.: Bergin and Garvey, 1985.

Atlas, James. "Beyond Demographics: How Madison Avenue Knows Who You Are and What You Want." *Atlantic Monthly*, October 1984, 49–58.

Auden, W. H. *For the Time Being*. London: Faber and Faber, 1945.

Auletta, Ken. "Annals of Communication: What Won't They Do?" *New Yorker*, 17 May 1993, 45–53.

Bagdikian, Ben H. "The Lords of the Global Village." *The Nation*, 12 June 1989, 805–20.

Baudrillard, Jean. *Simulations*. New York: Semiotext(e), 1983.

Baum, Gregory. "The Dumont Report." In *The Tabu of Democracy within the Church*, ed. James Provost and Knut Walf, 106–13. Concilium Series. London: SCM, 1992.

———. *Truth beyond Relativism: Karl Mannheim's Sociology of Knowledge*. Milwaukee: Marquette University Press, 1977.

Bell, Catherine. "The Ritual Body and the Dynamics of Ritual Power." *Journal of Ritual Studies* 4, no. 2 (1990): 299–313.

Berlin, Isaiah. "On Political Judgment," *New York Review*, 3 October 1996, 26–30.

Bernstein, Richard. *Beyond Objectivism and Relativism: Science, Hermeneutics, and Praxis*. Philadelphia: University of Pennsylvania Press, 1983.

Bourdieu, Pierre. *Distinction: A Social Critique of the Judgement of Taste*. Cambridge: Harvard University Press, 1984.

———. "The Economics of Linguistic Exchanges." *Social Science Information* 16, no. 6 (1977): 645–68.

———. *In Other Words: Essays towards a Reflexive Sociology*. Trans. Matthew Adamson. Stanford: Stanford University Press, 1990.

———. "Le Langage Autorisé: note sur les conditions sociales de l'efficacité du discours rituel." *Actes de la recherche en sciences sociales* (November 1975): 183–90.

———. *The Logic of Practice*. Trans. Richard Nice. Stanford: Stanford University Press, 1990.

———. *Outline of a Theory of Practice*. New York: Cambridge University Press, 1977.

Bowles, Samuel, and Herbert Gintis. "The Economy Produces the People: Introduction to Post-Liberal Democracy." In *Religion and Economic Justice*, ed. Michael Zweig, 221–44. Philadelphia: Temple University Press, 1991.

Brennan, Patrick J. *Parishes That Excel: Models of Excellence in Education, Ministry, and Evangelization*. New York: Crossroad, 1992.

Brueggemann, Walter. "Textuality in the Church." In *Tensions between Citizenship and Discipleship: A Case Study*, ed. Nelle G. Slater, 48–68. New York: Pilgrim Press, 1989.

Bruner, Jerome. *The Culture of Education*. Cambridge: Harvard University Press, 1996.

Buchler, Justus. *Toward a General Theory of Human Judgment*. New York: Columbia University Press, 1961.

Burton-Christie, Douglas. *The Word in the Desert: Scripture and the Quest for Holiness in Early Christian Monasticism*. New York: Oxford University Press, 1993.

Canadian Conference of Catholic Bishops. *Ethical Choices and Political Challenges: Ethical Reflections on the Future of Canada's Socio-Economic Order*. Ottawa: Canadian Conference of Catholic Bishops, 1984.

Capelle, D. "L'Introduction du catechumenat a Rome." *Recherches de théologie ancienne et médievale* 5 (1933): 151.

Chopp, Rebecca. *The Power to Speak: Feminism, Language, God*. New York: Crossroad, 1989.

Coles, Robert, and George Abbott White. "The Religion of the Privileged Ones." *Cross Currents* 31, no. 1 (1981): 1–14.

Collins, Mary. "Critical Questions for Liturgical Theology." *Worship* 53, no. 4 (1979): 302–17.

Comstock, Gary David. "The Houseguesting of Gay Scholars." *Council of Societies for the Study of Religion Bulletin* 23, no. 2 (April 1994): 35–37.

Congregation for the Evangelization of Peoples. *Guide for Catechists*. Rome, 1993.

Denby, David. "Buried Alive: Our Children and the Avalanche of Crud." *New Yorker*, 15 July 1996, 48–58.

Donald, James. Review of *Privacy and Publicity: Modern Architecture as Mass Media*, by Beatriz Colomina. *Media, Culture and Society* 18 (1996): 161–63.

Dudley, Carl. "Using Church Images for Commitment, Conflict, and Renewal." In *Congregations: Their Power to Form and Transform*, ed. C. Ellis Nelson, 89–113. Atlanta: John Knox, 1988.

Duffy, Eamon. *The Stripping of the Altars: Traditional Religion in England 1400–1580*. New Haven: Yale University Press, 1992.

Duffy, Regis. *On Becoming a Catholic: The Challenge of Christian Initiation*. San Francisco: Harper and Row, 1984.

Dunne, Joseph. *Back to the Rough Ground: "Phronesis" and "Techne" in Modern Philosophy and in Aristotle*. Notre Dame, Ind.: University of Notre Dame Press, 1993.

———. "What's the Good of Education?" In *Partnership and the Benefits of Learning: A Symposium on Philosophical Issues of Educational Policy*, ed. Padraig Hogan, 60–82 and 157–59. Maynooth, Ireland: Educational Studies Association of Ireland, 1995.

Dupanloup, Felix. *The Ministry of Catechizing*. London and Sydney: Griffith, Farran, Okeden and Welsh, 1890.

Dykstra, Craig. "Reconceiving Practice." In *Shifting Boundaries: Contextual Approaches to the Structure of Theological Education*, ed. Edward Farley and Barbara G. Wheeler, 35–66. Louisville: Westminster/John Knox, 1991.

Ellul, Jacques. *The Subversion of Christianity*. Grand Rapids: Eerdmans, 1986.

Eskenazi, Gerald. "The Male Athlete and Sexual Assault." *New York Times*, 3 June 1990, L1, L4.

Evans, Donald. *Struggle and Fulfillment*. New York: Collins, 1979.

Ewen, Stuart. *All-Consuming Images: The Politics of Style in Contemporary Culture*. New York: Basic Books, 1988.

Farley, Edward. *Ecclesial Reflection: An Anatomy of Theological Method*. Philadelphia: Fortress, 1982.

———. "Interpreting Situations: An Inquiry into the Nature of Practical Theology." In *Formation and Reflection: The Promise of Practical Theology*, ed. Lewis S. Mudge and James N. Poling, 1–35. Philadelphia: Fortress, 1987.

———. *Theologia: The Fragmentation and Unity of Theological Education*. Philadelphia: Fortress, 1983.

———. "Theology and Practice outside the Clerical Paradigm." In *Practical Theology*, ed. Don S. Browning, 21–41. San Francisco: Harper and Row, 1983.

Fasching, Darrell J. *Narrative Theology after Auschwitz: From Alienation to Ethics*. Minneapolis: Fortress, 1992.

Felman, Shoshana. "Psychoanalysis and Education: Teaching Terminable and Interminable." *Yale French Studies* 63 (1982): 21–44.

Finn, Thomas M. "Ritual Process and the Survival of Early Christianity: A Study of the Apostolic Tradition of Hippolytus." *Journal of Ritual Studies* 3, no. 1 (winter 1989): 69–89.

Fiorenza, Francis Schüssler. "The Church as a Community of Interpretation: Political Theology between Discourse Ethics and Hermeneutical Reconstruction." In *Habermas, Modernity, and Public Theology*, ed. Don S. Browning and Francis Schüssler Fiorenza, 66–91. New York: Crossroad, 1992.

————. "The Crisis of Hermeneutics and Christian Theology." In *Theology at the End of Modernity*, ed. Sheila Greeve Davaney, 117–40. Philadelphia: Trinity Press International, 1991.

————. *Foundational Theology*. New York: Crossroad, 1984.

————. "Foundational Theology and Theological Education." *Theological Education* (spring 1984): 107–24.

————. "Foundations of Theology: A Community's Tradition of Discourse and Practice." *Catholic Theological Society of America Proceedings* 41 (1986): 107–34.

————. "Theological and Religious Studies: The Contest of the Faculties." In *Shifting Boundaries: Contextual Approaches to the Structure of Theological Education*, ed. Edward Farley and Barbara G. Wheeler, 119–49. Louisville: Westminster/John Knox, 1991.

————. "Theory and Practice: Theological Education as a Reconstructive, Hermeneutical, and Practical Task." *Theological Education Supplement* (1987): 113–41.

Fosdick, Harry Emerson. *Great Voices of the Reformation: An Anthology*. New York: Modern Library, 1952.

Fraser, Kennedy. *The Fashionable Mind*. Boston: David R. Godine, 1985.

————. "Piper Pipe That Song Again." Review of *Blake*, by Peter Ackroyd. *New Yorker*, 27 May 1996, 126–31.

Freedberg, David. *The Power of Images: Studies in the History and Theory of Response*. Chicago: University of Chicago Press, 1989.

Geertz, Clifford. "Learning with Bruner," Review of *The Culture of Education*, by Jerome Bruner. *New York Review of Books*, 10 April 1997, 22–24.

Girard, René. *Things Hidden since the Foundation of the World*. Research undertaken in collaboration with Jean-Michel Oughourlian and Guy Lefort. Trans. Stephen Bann (bks. 2 and 3) and Michael Metteer (bk. 1). Stanford: Stanford University Press, 1987.

Gladwell, Malcolm. "A Reporter at Large: The Science of Shopping." *New Yorker*, 4 November 1996, 66–75.

Goldberger, Paul. "25 Years of Unabashed Elitism." *New York Times*, 2 February 1992, H1, H34.

Goldsmith, Barbara. "The Meaning of Celebrity." *New York Times Magazine*, 4 December 1983, 75 ff.

Goleman, Daniel. "Marriage Research Reveals Ingredients of Happiness." In *Perspectives on Marriage: A Reader*, ed. Kieran Scott and Michael Warren, 249–53. New York: Oxford University Press, 1993.

Greeley, Andrew. *A Theology of Culture*. Chicago: Thomas More, 1988.

Grosz, Elizabeth. *Sexual Subversions: Three French Feminists*. Boston: Allen and Unwin, 1989.

Gutiérrez, Gustavo. *The Power of the Poor in History*. Maryknoll, N.Y.: Orbis, 1983.

————. *A Theology of Liberation*. Trans. Caridad Inda and John Eagleson. Maryknoll, N.Y.: Orbis, 1973.

Habermas, Jürgen. *The Theory of Communicative Action.* Vol. 2, *Lifeworld and System: A Critique of Functionalist Reason.* Trans. Thomas McCarthy. Boston: Beacon Press, 1989.

Haight, Roger. "Critical Witness: The Question of Method." In *Faithful Witness: Foundations of Theology for Today's Church,* ed. Leo J. O'Donovan and T. Howland Sanks, 185–204. New York: Crossroad, 1989.

Hauerwas, Stanley. "The Church as God's New Language" and "The Gesture of a Truthful Story." In *Christian Existence Today.* Durham, N.C.: Labyrinth Press, 1988.

————. *In Good Company: The Church as Polis.* Notre Dame, Ind.: University of Notre Dame Press, 1995.

Hauerwas, Stanley, and David Burrell. "From System to Story: An Alternative Pattern for Rationality in Ethics." In *Why Narrative? Readings in Narrative Theology,* ed. Stanley Hauerwas and L. Gregory Jones, 158–90. Grand Rapids: Eerdmans, 1989.

Horton, Miles, and Paulo Freire. *We Make the Road by Walking: Conversations on Education and Social Change.* Ed. Brenda Bell et al. Philadelphia: Temple University Press, 1990.

Hurd, Bob. "Liturgy and Empowerment: The Restoration of the Liturgical Assembly." In *That They Might Live: Power, Empowerment, and Leadership in the Church,* ed. Michael Downey, 130–44. New York: Crossroad, 1991.

Hutter, Reinhard. "The Church as Public: Dogma, Practice, and the Holy Spirit." *Pro Ecclesia* 3, no. 3 (summer 1994): 334–61.

————. "Ecclesial Ethics, the Church's Vocation, and Paraclesis." *Pro Ecclesia* 2, no. 4 (fall 1993): 433–50.

Huxtable, Ada Louise. "Inventing American Reality." *New York Review of Books,* 3 December 1992, 24–29.

Jaeckle, Charles, and William A. Clebsch, eds. *Pastoral Care in Historical Perspective.* New York: Jason Aronson, 1975.

Jameson, Frederic. "Postmodernism, or the Cultural Logic of Late Capitalism." *New Left Review* 146 (July–August 1984): 53–92.

Jay, Martin. *The Dialectical Imagination.* Boston: Little Brown, 1973.

John Paul II. Discourse to the bishops of Zaire, 12 April 1983, no. 5: *Acta apostolicae sedis* 75 (1983): 620.

Joncas, Jan Michael. "The Public Language of Ministry Revisited: *de Ordinatione Episcopi, Presbyterorum et Diaconorum* 1990." *Worship* 68, no. 5 (September 1994): 386–403.

————. "Solemnizing the Mystery of Wedded Love: Nuptial Blessings in the *Ordo Celebrandi Matrimonium* 1991." *Worship* 70, no. 3 (May 1996): 210–37.

Juster, F. Thomas, and Frank P. Stafford, eds. *Time, Goods, and Well-Being.* Ann Arbor: University of Michigan Institute for Social Research, 1985.

Kavanaugh, John. "The World of Wealth and the Gods of Wealth." In *Option for the Poor: Challenge to the Rich Countries,* ed. L. Boff and V. Elizondo, 17–23. Concilium 187. Edinburgh: T. and T. Clark, 1986.

Kellner, Doug. "Postmodernism as Social Theory." *Theory, Culture, and Society* 5 (1988): 239–69.

Kierkegaard, Søren. *Purity of Heart Is to Will One Thing: Spiritual Preparation for the Office of Confession.* Trans. Douglas V. Steere. New York: Harper Torchbooks, 1956.

Komonchak, Joseph. "Clergy, Laity, and the Church's Mission in the World." *The Jurist* 41 (1981): 422–47.

————. "Ecclesiology and Social Theory." *The Thomist* 45 (1981): 283.

Lakeland, Paul. *Theology and Critical Theory: The Discourse of the Church.* Nashville: Abingdon, 1990.

Lévinas, Emmanuel. *Nine Talmudic Readings.* Bloomington: University of Indiana Press, 1994.

Levinson, Daniel. *The Seasons of a Man's Life.* New York: Knopf, 1978.

Levinson, Daniel, with Judy D. Levinson. *The Seasons of a Woman's Life.* New York: Knopf, 1996.

Little, Lester K. "Evangelical Poverty, the New Money Economy, and Violence." In *Poverty in the Middle Ages,* ed. David Flood, 11–26. Werl/Westfl., Germany: Dietrich-Coelde-Verlag, 1975.

————. *Religious Poverty and the Profit Economy in Medieval Europe.* Ithaca, N.Y.: Cornell University Press, 1978.

Lonergan, Bernard. "The Ongoing Genesis of Methods." *Studies in Religion* 6, no. 4 (1976–77): 341–55.

————. "The Transition from a Classicist Worldview to Historical-Mindedness." In *A Second Collection,* ed. William Ryan and Bernard Tyrrell, 1–9. Philadelphia: Westminster, 1974.

MacIntyre, Alisdair. *After Virtue.* Notre Dame, Ind.: University of Notre Dame Press, 1981.

MacKinnon, Catharine. "Pornography, Civil Rights, and Speech." *Harvard Civil Rights–Civil Liberties Law Review* 20 (1985): 1–70.

Macmurray, John. *Persons in Relation.* London: Faber and Faber, 1961.

Margolick, David. "Ignorance of L.A. Law Is No Excuse." *New York Times,* 6 May 1990, H27, H29.

McCarthy, Thomas. *The Critical Theory of Jürgen Habermas.* Cambridge: MIT Press, 1978.

Medvedev, P. N., and M. M. Bakhtin. *The Formal Method in Literary Scholarship.* Ed. Albert J. Wehrle. Baltimore: Johns Hopkins University Press, 1978.

Metz, Johann Baptist. "Productive Noncontemporaneity." In *Observations on "The Spiritual Situation of the Age,"* ed. Jürgen Habermas, 169–77. Cambridge: MIT Press, 1984.

————. "With the Eyes of a European Theologian." In *The Voice of the Victims,* ed. L. Boff and V. Elizondo, 113–19. Concilium Series. London: SCM, 1990.

Meyrowitz, Joshua. *No Sense of Place: The Impact of Electronic Media on Social Behavior.* New York: Oxford University Press, 1986.

Miles, Margaret R. *Image as Insight: Visual Understanding in Western Christianity and Secular Culture.* Boston: Beacon Press, 1985.

————. *Practicing Christianity: Critical Perspectives for an Embodied Spirituality.* New York: Crossroad, 1988.

Nelson, C. Ellis. *How Faith Matures.* Louisville: Westminster/John Knox, 1989.

————. *Where Faith Begins.* Atlanta: John Knox, 1967.

————, ed. *Congregations: Their Power to Form and Transform.* Atlanta: John Knox, 1988.

————. "Some Educational Aspects of Conflict." In *Tensions between Citizenship and Discipleship: A Case Study,* ed. Nelle G. Slater. New York: Pilgrim Press, 1989.

Orsy, Ladislaus. "New Era of Participation in Church Life." *Origins* 17, no. 46 (28 April 1988): 796–800.

O'Sullivan, Chris. "Campus Rape Is Usually Fraternity-Related" (letter to the editor). *New York Times,* 5 December 1990, A26.

Palmer, Parker. *The Company of Strangers: Christians and the Renewal of America's Public Life.* New York: Crossroad, 1983.

Paul VI. *Apostolic Exhortation, "Evangelii Nuntiandi"* [On evangelization in the modern world]. Washington, D.C.: United States Catholic Conference, 1976.

Peirce, Charles Sanders. "How to Make Our Ideas Clear." In *Writings of Charles Sanders Peirce: A Chronological Edition.* Vol. 3 (1872–78), 257–75. Bloomington: Indiana University Press, 1986.

Pieris, Aloysius. *An Asian Theology of Liberation.* Maryknoll, N.Y.: Orbis, 1988.

————. "Christianity and Buddhism in Core-to-Core Dialogue." *Cross Currents* 37, no. 1 (spring 1987): 47–75.

————. *Love Meets Wisdom: A Christian Experience of Buddhism.* Maryknoll, N.Y.: Orbis, 1988.

————. "To Be Poor as Jesus Was Poor." *The Way* (July 1984): 186–97.

————. "Towards an Asian Theology of Liberation: Some Religio-Cultural Guidelines." *East Asian Pastoral Review* 16, no. 4 (1979): 206–30.

Pogrebin, Robin. "Magazines Learning to Take Not-So-Clueless (and Monied) Teenagers More Seriously." *New York Times,* 4 November 1996, D8.

Poster, Mark, ed. *Jean Baudrillard: Selected Writings.* Stanford: Stanford University Press, 1988.

Power, David N. "Households of Faith in the Coming Church." *Worship* 57, no. 3 (May 1983): 237–54.

————. "Power and Authority in Early Christian Centuries." In *That They Might Live: Power, Empowerment, and Leadership in the Church,* ed. Michael Downey, 25–38. New York: Crossroad, 1991.

Rahner, Karl. *Foundations of Christian Faith.* New York: Seabury, 1978.

Ricoeur, Paul. *Oneself as Another.* Chicago: University of Chicago Press, 1992.

Rothenberg, Randall. "The Media Business, Advertising: Panel Spurs Dispute over Alcohol Ads." *New York Times,* 2 December 1988, D14.

————. "Study Shows Power of Public-Service Ads." *New York Times*, 8 April 1991, D8.

Sawicki, Marianne. *The Gospel in History: Portrait of a Teaching Church.* New York: Paulist, 1988.

————. "Recognizing the Risen Lord." *Theology Today* 44, no. 4 (1988): 441–49.

————. *Seeing the Lord: Resurrection and Early Christian Practices.* Minneapolis: Fortress, 1994.

Schillebeeckx, Edward. *Church: The Human Story of God.* New York: Crossroad, 1990.

Schneiders, Sandra. "Living Word or Dead(ly) Letters: The Encounter between the New Testament and Contemporary Experience." *Catholic Theological Society of America Proceedings* 47 (1992): 45–60.

————. "Scripture as the Word of God." *Princeton Seminary Review* 14, no. 1 (February 1993): 18–35.

————. "Theology and Spirituality: Strangers, Rivals, or Partners?" *Horizons* 13, no. 2 (1986): 253–74.

Scott, Kieran, and Michael Warren. *Perspectives on Marriage: A Reader.* New York: Oxford University Press, 1993.

Searle, Mark. "Renewing the Liturgy — Again." *Commonweal*, 18 November 1988, 617–22.

Segundo, Juan Luis. *The Liberation of Dogma.* Maryknoll, N.Y.: Orbis, 1992.

Shea, William M. "Catholic Reaction to Fundamentalism." *Theological Studies* 57 (1996): 264–85.

Siebert, Charles. "The Cuts That Go Deeper." *New York Times Magazine*, 7 July 1996, 19–25 ff.

Slater, Nelle G., ed. *Tensions between Citizenship and Discipleship: A Case Study.* New York: Pilgrim Press, 1989.

Sloyan, Gerard S. "Piety Centered on Jesus' Sufferings and Some Eccentric Christian Understandings of the Mystery of Calvary." *Worship* 67, no. 2 (March 1993): 98–123.

Talk of the Town. *New Yorker*, 9 September 1991, 26–27. Tertullian, "On Penitence." In *Treatises on Penance*, trans. W. Le Saint, 24–26. Westminster, Md.: Newman, 1959.

Thistlethwaite, Susan Brooks, and Mary Potter Engel, eds. *Lift Every Voice: Constructing Christian Theologies from the Underside.* San Francisco: HarperSanFrancisco, 1990.

Torres, Carlos Alberto. *The Church, Society, and Hegemony: A Critical Sociology of Religion in Latin America.* Trans. Richard A. Young. London and Westport, Conn.: Praeger, 1992.

Touraine, Alain. *Return of the Actor: Social Theory in Postindustrial Society.* Trans. Myrna Godzich. Minneapolis: University of Minnesota Press, 1988.

Vincie, Catherine. "Gender Analysis and Christian Initiation." *Worship* 69, no. 6 (November 1995): 505–30.

————. "The Liturgical Assembly: Review and Reassessment." *Worship* 67, no. 2 (1993): 123–44.

Wainwright, Geoffrey. *Doxology: The Praise of God in Worship, Doctrine, and Life.* New York: Oxford University Press, 1980.

Warren, Michael. *Faith, Culture, and the Worshiping Community: Shaping the Practice of the Local Church.* Washington, D.C.: Pastoral Press, 1993.

————. "Judging the Electronic Communications Media." *Living Light* 31, no. 2 (winter 1994–95): 54–64.

————. *Seeing through the Media: A Religious View of Communications and Cultural Analysis.* Valley Forge, Pa.: Trinity Press International, 1997.

————. *Youth, Gospel, Liberation.* 3d ed. Dublin: Veritas, 1998.

————, ed. *Sourcebook for Modern Catechetics.* Winona, Minn.: St. Mary's Press, vol. 1, 1983; vol. 2, 1997.

Welch, Sharon D. *A Feminist Ethic of Risk.* Minneapolis: Augsburg, 1990.

Weschler, Lawrence. *A Miracle, a Universe: Settling Accounts with Torturers.* New York: Penguin, 1990.

Wheeler, Barbara G. "Uncharted Territory: Congregational Identity and Mainline Protestantism." In *The Presbyterian Predicament: Six Perspectives,* ed. M. J. Coalter, J. M. Mulder, and L. B. Weeks, 67–89. Louisville: John Knox, 1990.

Williams, Lena. "Women's Image in a Mirror: Who Defines What She Sees?" *New York Times,* 6 February 1992, A1, B7.

Williams, Raymond. "Means of Communication as Means of Production." In *Problems in Materialism and Culture,* 50–63. London: Verso Editions, 1980.

Wind, James P., and James W. Lewis. *American Congregations.* 2 vols. Chicago: University of Chicago Press, 1994.

Wyschogrod, Edith. *Saints and Postmodernism: Revisioning Moral Philosophy.* Chicago: University of Chicago Press, 1990.

Yoder, John Howard. *The Priestly Kingdom: Social Ethics as Gospel.* Notre Dame, Ind.: University of Notre Dame Press, 1984.

Index